What a Character!

INVENTORS & SCIENTISTS

Notable Lives from History

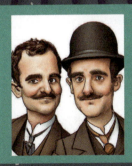

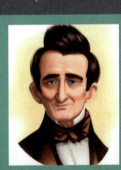

Marilyn Boyer

First printing: September 2023

Copyright © 2023 by Marilyn Boyer and Master Books. All rights reserved. No part of this book may be reproduced, copied, broadcast, stored, or shared in any form whatsoever without written permission from the publisher, except in the case of brief quotations in articles and reviews. For information write:

Master Books, P.O. Box 726, Green Forest, AR 72638

Master Books® is a division of the New Leaf Publishing Group, LLC.

ISBN: 978-1-68344-343-8
ISBN: 978-1-61458-869-6 (digital)
Library of Congress Control Number: 2023942195

Cover: Diana Bogardus
Interior: Terry White

Scripture taken from the New King James Version®. Copyright © 1982 by Thomas Nelson. Used by permission. All rights reserved.

Please consider requesting that a copy of this volume be purchased by your local library system.

Printed in the United States of America

Please visit our website for other great titles:
www.masterbooks.com

For information regarding promotional opportunities, please contact the publicity department at pr@nlpg.com.

Table of Contents

1. Carl Linnaeus — The Boy Who Loved Plants 5
2. Eli Whitney — Creative Inventor 15
3. Robert Fulton — Inventor of the Steamboat 25
4. Samuel F.B. Morse — A Man Who Wrote with Lightning 39
5. Louis Pasteur — The Boy Who Asked Questions 51
6. Alexander Graham Bell and the Talking Machine 59
7. Thomas Edison — Just the Strange Boy the World Needed 69
8. Booker T. Washington — From Slavery to Triumph 77
9. George Washington Carver — God's Plant Doctor 87
10. The Wright Brothers — Masters of Flight 99
Glossary 111
Corresponding Curriculum 115
Endnotes 117

All images are AI-generated shutterstock.com

Carl Linnaeus – The Boy Who Loved Plants

| 1707–1778 | A famous scientist who lived in Sweden |

Who Was Carl Linnaeus?

Carl Linnaeus was both an outstanding scientist and a **biblical creationist**, believing what the Bible tells us in the Book of Genesis. He lived in the 1700s and he is most famous for developing an orderly system for classifying animals and plants.

> **biblical creationist:** A scientist who believed the world was created by God in six days

It may seem strange that things like rocks and flowers would drive someone to leave his home to risk his life in wild and faraway places. Yet, when God wants to give a great gift to the world, He sometimes chooses unusual ways of sending the gift.

This was what happened in the life of Carl Linnaeus (Lin•a•us). Starting as a small child who liked flowers, Carl developed a passion to explore the wonders of creation. This great hunger to know would take him both into the world of books and on some amazing and dangerous adventures.

In the Garden

Carl was born in 1707 in Rashult, Sweden, in a farmhouse, to parents who both loved flowers. His father was the pastor of the local church and was a highly educated man and Carl was raised with a deeply religious upbringing. Both his father and mother hoped that their son would one day be a preacher like his father. It seemed that something in baby Carl was drawn to the beauty of God's creation, and his parents found that when he was upset, he calmed down when they gave him flowers.

As soon as he could walk, he wanted to totter outdoors and play with the plants. When he learned to talk, he wanted his father to teach him the name of every one.

Like a true adventurer, Carl was also fascinated by the bugs. There were so many different types: Big-eyed bugs. Crawling bugs. Flying bugs. Fuzzy bugs. Bugs with stripes. Bugs with spots. Bugs with many legs. What were the names of all these bugs? Bugs were so much more interesting than learning Greek and Latin. Carl's parents always knew where to find him when they noticed he had left his studies and disappeared. He would be in the garden.

Carl started school with the other children, but he proved to be a problem to the teachers. He just couldn't keep his mind on his books. He wanted to be outside studying the living things there. Some of his teachers told Rev. and Mrs. Linnaeus that their son would never be a minister. He just wasn't smart enough for all the studies the ministry required. The best thing would be to **apprentice** Carl to a tradesman. He might make a good shoemaker or **tanner**, they said. But he would never be a good minister.

Thankfully, there was one special teacher in the school who saw something in Carl that the other teachers did not. He saw that the boy's love of plants could be very useful. Carl should study to become a doctor!

apprentice: To work for a skilled craftsman to learn the trade

tanner: A person who tans animal hides to create leather

Medical School

When Carl's father thought about this, he realized that the teacher might be right. In those days, most medicines were made out of plants.

Doctors had to like plants and know a lot about them in order to take care of sick people. Carl thought it was a good idea as well. He could help people, make a living for himself, and still spend lots of time outdoors with bugs and flowers. Could he go to medical school?

Reverend Linnaeus was wise enough to know that people tend to be good at things they enjoy doing. Perhaps medical school would be a good choice for his son. But how would he pay for his schooling? Carl's parents were not wealthy. He would have to work to support himself and pay his school bills. Carl wanted very badly to study to be a doctor, so finally, his father and mother agreed.

It was hard for the young man. In 1727, he began his studies at Lund University at Lund, Sweden. He took whatever work he could find to earn a little money. He was often hungry. His shoes wore out and he put paper inside them to protect his feet, but he was determined. He worked hard and studied hard. Soon he was using his beloved plants to help sick people get well.

One of the problems of curing people with plants was in knowing what to name them. People did not agree on what plants were called. Some plants had 30 or more names! Depending on the town you lived in, you might call a dandelion a blow ball, a yellow daisy, or a **swine's** snout, or something else.

swine: Pig

Carl also discovered that dog bites could be treated using a pretty pink rose. He noticed that not all roses are the same, so it was hard to tell different doctors which rose he was using. Each doctor had his own long, Latin name for any type of rose.

It was just as bad with the animal kingdom. Scientists like to argue about whether a whale was a fish or a bat was a bird. Carl was frustrated by all the confusion. Somebody needed to figure out a system to name all the types of animals so that everyone could know what everyone else was talking about.

God's creation was so huge! There were millions of living things on earth — dogs, cats, horses, worms, flowers, jellyfish, ladybugs. Who could ever create a system to name them all and group them together with other organisms like them?

God's Hand in It All

It was a challenging problem, yet Carl saw God's hand in the great variety of creation. It was amazing! It was beautiful! He once said, "As one sits here in summertime and listens to the cuckoo and all the other bird songs, the crackling and buzzing of insects, as one gazes at the shining colors of flowers, doth one become **dumbstruck** before the Kingdom of the Creator."[1] Yes, God had made a beautiful world full of wonderful plants and animals. Even though Carl was young and just out of school, he would tackle the job.

dumbstruck: So surprised that one is unable to speak

First, he declared that all living things belonged in two kingdoms: the plant kingdom and the animal kingdom. He divided the two kingdoms into groups called classes. He divided plants into 24 classes, based on the different parts in their flowers. He gave each plant a Latin name.

But these Latin names would not be long and complicated. Oh no! A two-word name was enough to tell the plants apart. The names should be short and easy to remember. Safety pins, straight pins, bobby pins, hair pins. All were pins and it only took a two-word name to tell the difference. It should work for plants and animals too. The rose that healed dog bites would be *Rosa canina*: Dog rose. His first plant classification work was published in 1753.

It took a lot of time to decide on names for all the plants and animals he knew, but Carl was not satisfied. In other places, there were other creatures he had never seen. He published his first edition of his classification of animals in 1758.

The Uppsala Academy of Sciences paid for him to take journeys to faraway lands to learn about the plants and animals that lived there. Far to the north in **Lapland,** Carl searched out the natural wonders as he explored a harsh wilderness without roads. Sometimes he waded through icy water. Sometimes he nearly froze while searching for tiny mosses on his hands and knees. Treasures were to be found far above his head too, so Carl climbed trees to look for pinecones and nuts. Some of the plants he found had never been written about by scientists before.

> **Lapland:** A region in northern Norway, northern Sweden, and Northern Finland

All that he saw delighted him. The amazing variety of plants and animals, and the beauty of nature all around him, all reminded him of the greatness of the Creator. He once said: "Blessed be the Lord for the beauty of summer and spring, for the air, the water, the **verdure**, and the song of birds."[2] Yes, it was a big job he had undertaken, but the Creator deserved the best efforts the young scientist could offer.

verdure: Vegetation

Animals were just as interesting to Carl as plants. He wanted to choose names for them all and group them into classes. What a collection! Carl felt that living things had feelings. He was fascinated with things that ran or flew, crawled or swam. Among those creatures were eagles, catfish, raccoons, beetles, frogs, lions, elephants, snakes, and many more.

In the 1700s, scientists were confused about some animals. Some of them thought whales were fish and bats were birds. Carl studied them and discovered that bats and whales are both mammals. Birds have beaks but Carl, peeking into the mouths of bats found not beaks but teeth. Whales swim in the ocean as fish do, but they do not lay eggs as fish do. They bear their young live. They breathe air through lungs, not gills. It seemed very strange that whales were in the same group as bats, but Carl learned that they had much the same organs on the inside of their bodies.

As he had done with the plants, Carl gave each animal two names. He named dogs *Canis familiarus*. Then he moved on to the insect world. He looked at the differences and similarities between the insects, grouped them into groups, and gave names to the groups.

It would seem that other scientists would love Carl for all the work he had done. He had worked day and night with little time for rest or sleep. He made science simpler for everyone by organizing plants and animals with simple names that everyone could agree on. He went to the trouble of writing books to share his ideas with others. On the contrary, instead of praising him for his service to science, some people got angry.

Canis familiarus: Dog familiar

Famous scientists who had spent their lives studying plants and animals were not happy with Carl. Who was this young upstart who thought their long Latin names for things were useless? A botanist named Siegesbeck (syg•es•beckia) said that Carl's work was **"loathsome."** He wrote angry letters to Carl and Carl wrote angry letters in return. Finally, Carl paid Siegesbeck back for his hostility by naming a plant *Sigesbeckia orientalis*. The plant was an ugly, smelly weed.

loathsome: Repulsive or disgusting

An Interesting Teacher

When, in 1750, he was offered a job as a teacher at Uppsala University in Uppsala, Sweden, Carl accepted. He did not want his students to be bored and frustrated as he had been when he was a young scholar. He used his garden as a textbook. He had thousands of interesting plants for his pupils to study. In addition, he led them on field trips into the fields and woods. These were lively, exciting events lasting all day long. Sometimes he would take hundreds of students along. They traveled as in a parade, with musical instruments playing and banners flying. Whenever one of the students found a rare plant, he would order the bugles sounded to celebrate.

As years went by and his students became adults, some of them traveled to faraway lands to do nature studies, just as Carl had done in his youth. In China, Africa, Russia, Japan, India, and many other places they explored plant and animal life and taught people the ideas Carl had taught them.

From tropical jungles, blazing deserts, and snowy mountain peaks, these scientists sent thousands of plant and animal specimens for their teacher to name. It seemed his work of naming living things would never be done.

Eventually, Carl Linnaeus classified and named over 12,000 plant and animal species. Now, scientists around the world had a common language. Now they could all use the same name for a specimen whether they had grown up speaking German, English, Swedish, or Chinese. As the simple new system spread around the world, Carl became wealthy and famous. He was given many awards. Famous people and even kings and queens read his books. In 1757, the king of Sweden made Carl a knight — the first scientist ever to receive that honor.

Even with all this success, Carl did not retire and rest. He still kept busy in his garden, planting thousands of species from all around the world. Along with his plants, he enjoyed seeing his parrots, peacocks, and monkeys wandering among the beds and fountains at Uppsala, which became known as the Linnaean Gardens of Uppsala. He also kept on teaching others about the wonders of God's creation.

Quote by Linnaeus: "The observer of nature sees, with admiration, that 'the whole world is full of the glory of God.'" He further noted, "God infinite, omniscient and omnipotent, woke me up and I was amazed! I have read some clues through His created things, in all of which, is His will; even in the smallest things, and the most minute! How much wisdom! What an inscrutable perfection!"[3]

2
Eli Whitney – Creative Inventor

| 1765–1825 | American inventor |

Who Was Eli Whitney?

Eli Whitney was an American inventor, best remembered as the inventor of the cotton gin, but most importantly for developing the concept of mass production of interchangeable parts. He was born in 1765 in Westboro, Massachusetts. Eli prepared for Yale at Leicester Academy (now Becker College) and under the tutelage of Rev. Elizur Goodrich of Durham, Connecticut. Whitney attended Yale College and graduated in 1792.

The Watch

Ten-year-old Eli Whitney looked down at the dozens of tiny metal pieces on the table before him. He had really done it this time. Here was his father's prize silver watch, taken apart and scattered across the tabletop. It had been so easy to open the case and remove the little bits of metal that produced the steady tick-tick-tick that so fascinated a little boy. But now it was time to put all those little bits back together again. Could he do it? He swallowed hard. He was not sure anybody could do that.

The watch was just one more mechanical thing that drew Eli's attention like steel to a magnet. Born in 1765, and raised on the family farm in Westboro, Massachusetts, he had always been more interested in the farm workshop than what was growing in the fields. He examined all the farm equipment until he was sure he understood how it worked. He wanted to know how everything was made and what made it do its job. His restless mind could not be at peace until he solved each mystery.

That was why he had always wanted to examine his father's watch. It was so beautifully put together! So small and so shiny, so perfectly round. It ticked steadily all day and all night and all that his father did to make it keep on ticking was to wind it. What mysteries must be inside that silver circle! What magic it must contain!

He hadn't meant to take the watch all apart. He just wanted to get his hands on it — to pry off the back cover and look his fill at the marvels that must be between the two silver disks. And oh, how wonderful it was when he had done so! All those tiny wheels and levers, each mysteriously doing its little part to produce the wonderful, steady tick-tick-tick. But some parts were hidden by other parts. There was no way to see them but to remove some things. And now — he felt a queasy churning in his stomach.

How much time did he have? He had stayed home with his sick mother while Father took his brothers and sister to church. It was a good thing that church lasted a long time in those days. Still, surely there was no time to be wasted. Eli took a deep breath and began putting little pieces back in place, one by one. He hoped with all his heart that he was doing it right, but there were so many pieces. And some of them looked just like others. How could he be sure he was doing it right?

Finally, he placed the back cover on the watch and snapped it into place. Holding it carefully and hardly daring to breathe, he quietly walked into the living room. Nervously he listened for the hoof beats of his father's team returning from church. No sound came from the road. He set the watch to exactly the time showing on the big clock on the mantelpiece. Now, for the final test. He began to wind the spring as far as it would go. When the stem would turn no farther, Eli took his fingers off.

It worked! Joyously the little mechanic listened to the ticking. It seemed to him that it was the most beautiful sound he had ever heard. He could hardly believe that he had taken all those shiny little parts out of the watch and made them all go back into their proper places, but he had. It had been a frightening task, but he had done it. Now he would have more confidence than ever before in working with machines — even tiny ones with lots of parts.

An Inventor at Heart

Two years later, Eli was still at it. His sickly mother had died, and a housekeeper had been hired to help keep house. When Father had to be away for a few days, he returned and asked what his sons had been doing around their Connecticut farm in his absence. "Well," she replied, "one of the boys mended that stone wall between two fields. Another one hoed the onion patch."

"And what did Eli do?" his father wanted to know.

"He made a fiddle," was the reply.[4] The father sighed. The boy was not much of a farmer.

Instead, he was an inventor. The fiddle proved to be made much like other violins. The music it produced was fairly good. Everyone who saw it was amazed that it had been made by a 12-year-old boy. Soon fiddlers from all around were bringing their instruments to Eli when they needed fixing. He could usually take care of the problem.

When Eli was 14 years old, his father remarried. His new stepmother owned a beautiful set of knives which she said had been made in England. She said such fine knives could not be made in America.

"I could make them myself if I had the tools," Eli replied.[5] This sounded like foolish bragging to the rest of the family, but a few weeks later Eli got the chance to do just that. One of the fancy knives broke. Eli took the pieces of the knife to the workshop and went to work. With his clumsy set of tools, he produced a new knife. When he showed it to his stepmother she was amazed. The only way she could tell the difference between her knives and the new one was that the rest of the set was stamped with the **trademark** of the English maker.

Two years later, Eli's handyman skills started adding to the family's income. He became a nail maker. The Revolutionary War was underway and trade with England had stopped. Because there were no nail factories in America, nails had always been bought from England. Now they had to be made by hand if Americans were to get nails at all. Eli put his curious mind to work and quickly figured out how to make nails in his father's shop. Soon the Whitney family was selling nails by the hundreds.

trademark: A symbol or word legally registered to represent a company

With the end of the war, trade with the mother country began again. Now it was cheaper to buy nails from England than to pay for hand-made American nails. Eli's sales **tapered off** to a trickle. It was time to find another job.

tapered off: Slowed down

He turned back to his tools and began making walking sticks and hat pins for sale. He was successful again, partly because he had very high standards for his work. He would say, "Whatever is worth doing at all, is worth doing well."

Determination Pays Off

At the age of 19, Eli began longing to study other things. He decided to go to Yale College in New Haven. He lacked schooling, for he had never worked very hard studying books. He also lacked money. A college education was expensive, but Eli Whitney was a determined young man. He took some more schooling. He worked hard on the farm and in the shop. After a while, he was able to learn enough to get a job as a schoolteacher. Finally, at the age of 23, he went to Yale.

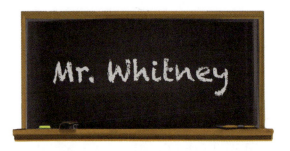

Eli had to work hard at his studies and also take on work to pay for his schooling. While at Yale he repaired a machine used in one of his classes. The teacher said it would have to be sent to England for repair, but when Eli offered to try to fix it, he was allowed to try. He succeeded as usual, and the professor was amazed.

After college, Eli set his sights on a career as a lawyer. But that would mean more years of study and more money for room and board. When he was offered a job teaching school in Georgia, he decided to take it. He had never seen the South. It would be interesting and he would escape the cold winters of Connecticut for a time.

When his ship stopped in New York, Eli met the wife of a very famous man. She was Mrs. Greene, the widow of General Nathaniel Greene of Washington's army. Mrs. Greene and her children were on their way home to their plantation, Mulberry Grove, near Savannah, Georgia. The widow quickly took a liking to the young man and found that her children soon came to love him. He was no ordinary young man. Before the trip was over, Eli and the Greene family had become very close friends.

But disappointment awaited young Whitney at Savannah. The job which had been offered to him was not what it had seemed. The salary was only half what he had been told it was. He had traveled all those hundreds of miles for a job he could not afford to accept!

Mrs. Greene came to his rescue. "Do not even think of taking the position," she said earnestly.[6] She invited him to come to Mulberry Grove and stay with her family until a better opportunity came his way. He could study law in the meantime, she told him. Eli accepted her kind offer.

He found Mulberry Grove to be a beautiful place. The house was a mansion, once owned by the **Tory** governor of Georgia before America won her freedom. He especially loved the library with its thousands of books. Here was a place where he could study happily until he found a job. The farm itself was also lovely, with broad fields and pretty fruit trees. Yes, Eli was glad he had turned down the deceitful offer from the school.

> **Tory:** American colonist who supported the British side

Eli Whitney — Creative Inventor

A Machine Is Needed

It was not long before Mrs. Greene discovered that Eli was a good mechanic. When her embroidery frame started tearing the cloth she was working on, he took it and told her he could make a better one. He did, and even though the new frame was of a very different design than the old one, it worked much better. The kindly widow was delighted and often told her visitors what a brilliant young man Mr. Whitney was.

One group of guests was eager to meet Eli when their hostess praised him to them. They were former army officers and local planters who had been discussing the problems of growing cotton in Georgia. A variety called short-staple cotton grew well in their red soil but was hard to use. The cotton seeds inside the bolls were hard to remove. They had to be picked out by hand so the cotton lint could be spun into cloth. This was a very slow process. It would take a worker several hours to clean a pound or two of cotton.

What they needed, the planters said, was a machine that could separate cotton from its seeds quickly. A machine like that could do more work in a day than a dozen men.

Mrs. Greene showed them her embroidery frame. "Gentlemen," she told her guests, "I have a friend who has just come from the North, a graduate of Yale College. He is a perfect genius at contriving machinery. Explain to him what is needed, and I'm sure he can help you."[7]

A servant called for Eli, and he happily went to meet the gentlemen. He eagerly listened as they explained their need for a new machine. Yes, he told them, he thought he could invent one. The planters were very excited and told him they would return after a while and check on his progress.

Weeks went by but the new machine had not been created. Eli needed money for materials to build his new "cotton gin" (short for engine) and he had none.

Mrs. Greene continued to believe in Eli. So did her farm manager, Mr. Miller. He offered to become Eli's partner and lend the money to start their new business. Soon Eli was hard at work in a workshop Mrs. Greene had set up in her basement. Eagerly, she and Mr. Miller watched his progress from day to day. No one else was allowed to see what Whitney was doing in the shop. He wanted to finish his machine and get a **patent** before anyone could see it and create their own cotton gin.

Finally, the first model was finished. It had little wire teeth on a cylinder that was turned by hand. The teeth pulled the cotton fibers off the seeds and the seeds dropped away. When the design had been perfected, Eli planned to build gins big enough to be turned by horses or by water power. He and Mr. Miller planned to gin the cotton themselves rather than sell the gins. They would let the farmers pay them in cotton. The farmers would keep most of the cotton and Whitney and Miller would keep the rest to sell.

> **patent:** A legal document protecting his invention from copycats

Things went wrong from the very first. Others heard how the gin worked and started building gins of their own using Whitney's ideas. Miller and Whitney went to court to protect their patent rights, but there were many imitators using their idea. It took 13 years of fighting in court to finally win protection for their patent. But patents only last for 14 years, so they had very little time to earn money for their invention.

Not all was lost. The cotton gin did make Eli Whitney famous. In 1798, when the United States needed thousands of rifles for their army, Whitney was able to get the job of making rifles. Again he put his creative mind to work and found better ways to make rifles. Instead of making the rifles one by one as they had always been, Eli made "interchangeable" parts. That meant that a part made for one of his rifles would fit any rifle made in his factory. Instead of needing an experienced gunsmith to make each rifle individually, he could hire unskilled men and teach them to quickly put together a rifle from his parts. It took several years to make his system work, but finally, Eli Whitney was selling rifles to the government by the thousands.

The wealth that had never come to Eli Whitney from the invention of the cotton gin finally caught up with him. His system of interchangeable parts produced rifles so quickly that he became a rich and famous man. Other types of factories also began to use his system to produce their products. In the years to come, Whitney's genius would make a tremendous difference in America. Now his ideas, such as how to manufacture muskets by machine so that the parts were interchangeable, would be used to produce the goods needed for a rapidly growing nation.

Robert Fulton – Inventor of the Steamboat

| 1765–1815 | American invented steamboat in 1807 |

Who Was Robert Fulton?

Robert Fulton invented the first commercially successful steamboat and brought the technology of steam power to the rivers of the United States. Fulton's steamboats helped to power the Industrial Revolution by moving 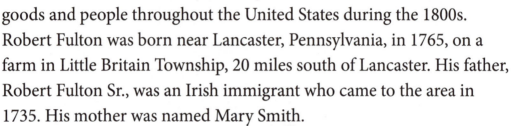 goods and people throughout the United States during the 1800s. Robert Fulton was born near Lancaster, Pennsylvania, in 1765, on a farm in Little Britain Township, 20 miles south of Lancaster. His father, Robert Fulton Sr., was an Irish immigrant who came to the area in 1735. His mother was named Mary Smith.

It was quiet that afternoon in the little Quaker schoolhouse in Lancaster, Pennsylvania. Only the sounds of shuffling feet, turning pages, and scratching quill pens could be heard until the schoolmaster left his high stool behind the desk and began to walk down the aisle. One by one, young heads went up to see what the master was doing. He was pacing toward the bench where one head was concentrating on a task and seemed to see or hear nothing else. Robert Fulton was drawing again. It appeared that he had forgotten where he was and what he was supposed to be doing.

A Head Full of Ideas

The teacher stopped and looked down with disapproval. Why could this boy never stick to his assignments until they were finished? Why must he always be distracted by some wild idea for a picture? Suddenly the boy noticed the master standing beside him. He knew he was in trouble, but oh, what a wonderful drawing he had made! Quickly he held it up for the master to see. His youthful face glowed with excitement as if to say, "Isn't this a fine picture?"

The drawing was indeed a good one. The teacher was truly impressed, so he did not scold the boy. He simply said, "It would be better for thee, Robert, to spend thy time studying thy books."[8]

The boy answered, "I know it, sir, but my head is so full of my own ideas that there seems to be no room in it for ideas from books."[9]

The teacher walked back to his desk and the children all wondered if he was about to seize his ruler and apply a reminder to Robert that schoolwork was the business to be minded at that hour of the day. No such thing happened, and they all soon returned their attention to their books, including Robert.

In school, Robert Fulton seemed a somewhat slow student, and his teacher sometimes grew impatient with him. Yet it was plain that Robert was a bright boy outside of school. He seemed very eager to learn all that he could learn by observing the world around him. One day he appeared at the school late, and everyone expected he would be punished. When the teacher asked the reason for his tardiness, he held up a lead pencil for the man to see. "I have been at the **smith's** pounding out lead for this pencil, and it is a good one, too," he replied honestly.[10]

smith: Blacksmith

This was in the 1770s, and pencils were very scarce. Goose quill pens were the common writing instrument then. Most of the children had never seen a pencil and the teacher had only seen a few. He looked over Robert's creation carefully, then took out a pen knife and sharpened the end of it. He wrote a few words on a sheet of paper with it, then handed it back. Instead of scolding or whipping the boy, the teacher praised him heartily for doing something so useful with his time. Soon the other students were begging Robert to make pencils for them, too.

Robert was considered to be one of the most promising boys in the town. He was good-natured and **witty**, quick to make friends, and pleasant to talk to. People liked him. He often visited the craftsmen's shops and passed the time with them, asking questions and watching as they did their work. Rather than being impatient with his questions, the men enjoyed talking with him and sometimes even let him use their tools to try his hand at the work. He was a quick learner — when the work was interesting to him — and before he reached his teen years he had acquired a remarkable amount of knowledge about mechanical things.

witty: Quick and inventive humor

As he grew older, Robert did better work in school. His papers were always neat and beautiful, and he had a gift for mathematics that surprised his teacher. He continued to draw whenever he had time to spare, and his art became better and better though he had never taken art lessons from anyone.

Fourth of July

When he was 11 years old, the American colonies went to war against England for their independence. Robert was much too young to join the army, but he was a loyal patriot. He rejoiced on July 4, 1776, when the Declaration of Independence was signed. He was glad when the event was celebrated with the firing of **muskets** and cannons. It delighted him to see the villages lit up until late at night by bonfires in the streets and candles glowing in all the house windows.

Two years later, just before the 4th of July in 1778, a notice was put up in Lancaster, asking the people not to light up their homes in celebration. Candles were scarce and should be saved for a time when they were needed. Robert was disappointed, but his active brain would not allow him to watch the glorious Fourth go by without some kind of celebration. After a while, an idea came to him. He gathered some gunpowder and **pasteboard** and disappeared into the barn for several hours.

musket: An infantryman's light gun with a long barrel, typically smooth-bored, muzzleloading, and fired from the shoulder

On the evening of the Fourth, he emerged from the barn carrying several long tubes with slender sticks attached to them. Robert had made rockets! This Fourth would be celebrated in Lancaster in a very notable way.

pasteboard: A type of thin board made by pasting together sheets of paper

Robert placed his rockets carefully and picked up a lighted candle. He touched the flame to the bottom of one of the rockets. Hiss! The gunpowder inside flashed and up went the rocket, high into the warm, dark sky. All over the town people looked up, startled. Was it a **meteor**? No, there went another blazing streak in a graceful arc across the sky. Then there was another. And another! No doubt this display was upsetting to the horses and cows in the neighborhood, but the glorious Fourth had not passed unnoticed in Lancaster. And the young inventor had used only one candle.

meteor: A shooting star

Robert combined his interest in gunpowder with his talent for art. Because the country was at war with England, many gun shops were open day and night. The army needed many guns, and Americans were determined that they should be provided. Young Fulton was fascinated by guns — as he was by anything mechanical — and he studied them carefully. He made beautiful drawings of guns, showing all the parts in detail. Sometimes he made drawings that showed ideas he thought would improve the guns and make them more effective. On occasion, the gunsmiths would try out his ideas. Often they found that Fulton's suggestions made their guns better.

His mathematical skill helped the gun makers, too. He could figure out how far a gun of certain measurements would shoot a ball. When the shop finished making the gun and it was tried out in the field, the men usually found that Robert's figures had been correct. And he was just a boy!

At 17, Robert decided that he was no longer a boy but a man. He started out to build his career. He had many interests, but most of all he wanted to be an artist. So he wrote to Benjamin West, the famous

American painter who at that time was living in England. West offered to help him learn to paint if he could come to London. On the way across the Atlantic, Robert noticed that the sailing ship he was on wasted considerable time sitting still when the wind was not blowing in the right direction. He wondered if he could find a better way to make ships go. It was an interesting problem, but it would have to wait for a while before Robert Fulton could work on it. He was on his way to becoming a famous artist.

Robert became a close friend of Benjamin West and learned much from him. West also introduced him to others who appreciated his painting, and so his group of friends grew. Like Robert, his new friends were interested in more things than just art. One was a wealthy duke who was interested in building canals. Canals were very important in those days before there were good roads. As the two men talked about the challenges of building canals, Robert realized that people in Pennsylvania needed canals as much as dukes in England.

Pennsylvania farmers produced good crops, but it was hard to get their corn and wheat to market. Roads were bad and wagons were small. If canals could be built across Pennsylvania, long boats could be built that would carry very large loads. As Robert thought about this problem, he began to see that if he could solve it, he would have helped a great many people. Perhaps this was more important than painting beautiful pictures for them.

From Art to Engineering

So it was that Robert Fulton gradually turned his attention away from art to engineering. But his artistic skills were not wasted. They helped him to put his ideas on paper so they could be studied and improved. In 1786, Fulton moved to Bath, Virginia, where his portraits and landscapes were so well-appreciated that his friends urged him to study art in Europe. Fulton returned to Philadelphia, where he hoped his paintings would attract a sponsor. Impressed by his art, and hoping to improve the city's cultural image, a group of local merchants paid Fulton's fare to London in 1787. Before he left England he invented several improvements in canals and the boats that traveled on them. He also invented a machine for spinning flax, a machine for clearing earth from canal beds, and a mill for cutting marble. When he left England for a time in France in 1797, he was well known as a man who was a genius at inventing things that made life better for others.

In France, Robert started studying again. He found that along with his many ideas, there was also room for foreign languages, science, and even more mathematics. He painted pictures to sell for enough money to live on. His driving passion, however, was inventing and improving useful things.

About to Change the World

When Robert Fulton returned to his native America in 1806, he brought back with him a good reputation, good health, good spirits, and good hopes. He also had a good supply of money that he had earned from his paintings. He was still a young man though he had many accomplishments behind him. The project that would make him famous and change the world was still ahead.

Another thing Robert brought home from Europe was a steam engine. People in various countries were experimenting with steam power, but so far no one had been very successful in making it useful. Robert's idea was a boat that would be driven by steam and so would not depend on the wind. No one had yet managed to make such a boat that worked well, but he was determined to be the first man to do so.

He had tried his idea in France. He made a small model steamboat that actually worked. But when he built a full-size boat and fitted it with a steam engine, things did not go as planned. In France, Fulton met Robert R. Livingston, an American lawyer, politician, and diplomat from New York, as well as a Founding Father of the United States, who was appointed as U.S. Ambassador to France in 1801. He also had a scientifically curious mind, and the two men decided to work together on building a steamboat and to try operating it on the **Seine** River. They had invited several **prominent** people to join them on their first voyage on the Seine River and were eagerly looking forward to a history-making day. The night before the trip, however, the boat broke in the middle and sank. The engine had been too heavy and the frame of the boat too weak.

Seine: A river in France

prominent: Famous, important

Fulton plunged into the river right along with his workmen. They raised the parts of the boat and found out what had happened. They went back to work on the frame design and built a better, stronger boat. Months later, the boat was launched on the Seine.

The boat, much to the amazement of many, began to move across the river. Black smoke billowed from the stacks, great paddle wheels churned the water and Fulton's heart swelled within him. He knew that at long last, he had won. Still, he was not satisfied. Everyone else considered the invention to be like a miracle, but the inventor knew there was plenty of room for improvement. The boat was too slow. They had improved the frame; now they would improve the engine.

Fulton's Folly to Success

He returned to America to perfect his boat. It was expensive to experiment with steam power, so he looked for wealthy people who would loan him money. Many of them could have made loans to him, but they did not have faith in his vision as he did himself. What a wild idea! For many thousands of years, people had traveled by water. They had paddled boats and poled boats. Boats had been pulled along canals by mules. The best way they had found to move a boat was with wind and sails, and that was how it had been done for centuries. What a dreamer this young Fulton was! His project became known as Fulton's Folly. It is amazing how God uses ordinary and sometimes misunderstood people to bring about much good for mankind. Such was the case with Robert Fulton.

There were a few wealthy men who thought the idea had a chance. Finally, Robert was able to order his new boat built at the Charles Brown shipyards. During the winter of 1806, most of his time was spent supervising the construction. Sometimes  people who did not know him would stop to look at the boat. With the designer standing right beside them, they would laugh at it and talk about how glad they were that they had not invested any of their money in such a silly scheme. This boat would go nowhere! It would probably sink. Or perhaps the engine would blow up and kill everybody on board. But there are always doubters who laugh at people with vision. Robert understood this and continued to work despite the criticism.

On a fair morning in the late summer of 1807, crowds gathered at a dock on the Hudson River to see the end of Fulton's Folly. Floating beside the dock they saw an ugly, box-like craft whose clumsy-looking smokestack poured clouds of black smoke. The ends of the boats had decks, but the middle was open, and the machinery was in plain view. Even Mr. Livingston, Robert's partner, described it as "a backwoods sawmill mounted on a scow and set on fire."[11]

The command was given to start. Big paddle wheels began to churn the blue water into foam. The jeering crowd on the dock grew silent. Would this weird thing work after all? It was working! A cheer went up from the group! It was working! Steadily the *Clermont*, moved out into the water. The people who had come to **jeer** and make fun of Fulton's Folly were suddenly transformed into admirers of the young engineer. They were watching history being made before their very eyes.

Then it stopped. People stopped cheering and held their breaths. The *Clermont* floated helplessly in the river, beginning to turn sideways across the current. The invited passengers on the boat began to look at each other fearfully. Would their great day end in humiliation?

Clermont: Fulton had named the ship, after Clermont, Mr. Livingston's beautiful estate

jeer: Make rude and mocking remarks

frantically: In a hurried, distraught manner

Fulton stood on a chair and begged his guests for patience. Just give him a few minutes to check the engine, he pleaded. Quickly he ran down to the engine and searched **frantically** for the problem. He found it and was relieved to see that it was a small one. Quickly he made the repair and returned to the deck. Again the great wheels turned and churned. Again the boat moved steadily and swiftly up the stream toward Albany. This time it kept going. The crowd on the bank returned to cheering, and the passengers on the boat waved their hats and handkerchiefs in reply. Soon they were out of hearing.

Now the gathering on the deck became a party. Smiles, handshakes, and words of congratulations flew from person to person. There were about 40 people on the boat, mostly well-known in New York society. Two were granddaughters of Mr. Livingston, invited by him so they could one day tell their children how they had been a part of making history. One was his cousin, Harriet Livingston, one of the outstanding beauties of that great family. Mr. Fulton was a delightful host, full of joy at his success and eager to share his joy with his guests. One of the ladies on board wrote to a friend later, "That son of a Pennsylvania farmer was a prince among men; as modest as he was great, and as handsome as he was modest. His eyes were glowing with love and genius."[12]

That maiden voyage changed history. From that day on, sail-powered travel was a relic whose days were numbered. Steam-driven ships would soon take over the seas and churn their way from nation to nation and continent to continent. Steamboats would paddle their thrashing way up and down the great rivers of the world. No more would the lack of a favorable wind keep those who go down to the sea in ships from keeping their scheduled appointments.

The day changed Robert Fulton's personal history, too. When the boat stopped for a visit at Clermont on that first trip to Albany, Robert's partner made an announcement: cousin Harriet Livingston was engaged to become Mrs. Robert Fulton.

Samuel F.B. Morse – A Man Who Wrote with Lightning

| 1791–1872 | American inventor |

Who Was Samuel F.B Morse?

Samuel Morse revolutionized communication by putting scientific knowledge to work. He is famous for inventing the **Morse code** and the **telegraph**. He did not see any conflict between his scientific knowledge and Christianity — in fact, quite the opposite. He believed that "education without religion is in danger of substituting wild theories for the simple commonsense rules of Christianity."[13] Samuel Finley Breese Morse was born in Charlestown, Massachusetts, on Wednesday April 27, 1791. He was educated at a Christian boarding school and then attended Yale College. Yale was established as a religious school as designated in its charter "wherein Youth may be instructed in the Arts & Sciences who through the blessing of Almighty God may be fitted for Publick employment both in Church and the Civil State."

> **Morse code:** An alphabet or code in which letters are represented by combinations of long and short signals of light or sound
>
> **telegraph:** A system for transmitting messages from a distance along a wire
>
> **Yale College:** Today's Yale University in New Haven, Connecticut

Days at Yale

When Samuel F.B. Morse showed up at **Yale College** in 1807, he appeared to be well-prepared for college life. He was mature for his age and had learned well from his teachers and his parents. His father was a congregational minister, a highly educated and respected man. His mother was a gracious lady who kept a tidy house and readily welcomed visitors of all classes. Finley, as he was called, had learned from his father to act with dignity, showing respect to others. From his mother, he had learned to be kind to others and make them feel comfortable around him. He was the sort of boy who was noticed by those around him and who made friends easily. His teachers liked him because he was respectful to them and studied hard. He was popular with his classmates and was active in college life.

He often wrote letters home to Charlestown, Massachusetts, telling his parents what life was like at Yale. He told them of a meteor that fell not far from the college. In another letter, he described a "trial" that the students held to punish the school's cooks for misusing college food, being rude to the students, and not keeping the cooking "clean" enough. His busy father found time to write back, encouraging Finley to keep writing often and to learn to be clear and effective in expressing himself in letters. As long as he lived, Dr. Morse would be a strong supporter of his son's work.

During Finley's senior year, both of his younger brothers joined him at Yale. They all kept up with their studies, yet they found time to have fun together. One day they sent up a huge hot air balloon from the college campus. They had made it from sheets of letter paper pasted together. Eighteen feet long, the airborne paper bag attracted quite a crowd of onlookers.

Finley was skillful with his fingers.

A natural artist, he spent many hours drawing faces and heads. The walls of his room were covered with pictures of his friends. As time went by, he enjoyed drawing more and more. Though he never had any formal art lessons, he gradually became able to draw very good likenesses simply through practice.

As photography had not been invented yet, many people wanted to have pictures made of themselves and their friends. Young Morse became so adept at drawing these portraits that in his last year of college he was able to pay part of his school expenses by charging a few dollars for a portrait. Although not a rich man, he always made generous donations to God's work. He supported missionaries and gave to institutions which trained clergymen. Morse gave his time to God as well. In his home church, he established one of the first Sunday Schools in the United States. Finley Morse made up his mind that he would pursue a career as an artist.

Yet another strong interest had sprung up in his mind while at Yale. Professor Day taught a class in natural philosophy, which we now call science. In this class, Finley first began learning about electricity. Benjamin Franklin experimented with electricity and proved by flying a kite in a rainstorm that lightning is electricity. Professor Day was also doing experiments and was eager to share them with his students.

Fascinated by Electricity

After one class, Professor Day told the students to form a circle and hold hands. Then one student touched the pole of an electric battery and at the same instant all the boys felt a slight shock flash through their bodies. Finley later described the shock as feeling like a slight blow across the shoulders. Next, the laboratory was darkened and a current of electricity was passed through an iron chain. As the students watched in wonder, they saw sparks of white light flash between the links of the chain. It was amazing!

Finley Morse was deeply impressed. He thought a power like electricity, traveling a distance almost instantly, could be put to some great use. He wrote home to his father and described the experiments to him. Then, when he could not afford to travel home during vacation time he spent much of that time doing electrical experiments in the laboratory himself. His inquiring mind enjoyed practicing the theories he had learned in the classroom.

These were the early days of America. There were not yet any good art schools in the young country, so young men who wanted to be artists usually went to Europe to study. Young Morse struck up a friendship with the famous painter Washington Allston in 1811 and made arrangements to spend a year in London with him as his student.

Days in London

It was more than a month after leaving America that Finley sat down to write to his parents and let them know that he had arrived safely. "I only wish you had this letter now … I can imagine Mother wishing that she could hear of my arrival and thinking of a thousand accidents

which may have befallen me. I wish that in an instant I could communicate the information; but three thousand miles are not passed over in an instant, and we must wait four long weeks before we can hear from each other."[14] Little did he know that one day his own invention would make such instant communication possible.

In London, Finley learned much from the teaching of Mr. Allston. He also became acquainted with another famous American painter, Benjamin West. West showed Finley some of his paintings. The king himself had praised West's paintings and had paid West to paint the king's portrait. When West saw Finley's eyes light up with joy while looking at West's art, the great painter quickly felt appreciation for the young man. He invited Finley to come to him at any time for help.

West and Allston saw much talent in their young pupil. They liked him and wanted to help him do his very best work. So, they set high standards for him and were critical of his efforts. Once Finley spent hours on a drawing, polishing the details and looking it over with a careful eye. When it was finished he was quite proud of it. He took it to Mr. West for his approval.

"It is a remarkable production, and you undoubtedly have talent, sir," the master said. "It will do you credit when it is finished."

"Finished!" Morse echoed with dismay. "It is finished."

"By no means," the artist replied. "See here and here and here." He pointed to various parts of the picture.

When he did so, Finley quickly saw that there were indeed some imperfections in his work. He took it home and worked on it for another week, then took it back to West.

Again, West found fault. "Look at this muscle and these finger joints."

Finley had to admit he was right. Back to his apartment he went to attack his problems once more. Once again West said, "Very good — go finish it."

Finley was deeply discouraged by this. "I have done my best," he said. "I can do no more."

West looked at his student kindly. "Very well," he said. "That is all I want. It is a splendid drawing. I might have accepted it as you presented it at first, but that was not your best work. You have learned more by finishing this one picture than you would have learned by drawing a dozen incomplete ones. Success lies not in the number of drawings but in the character of one. Finish one picture, and you are a painter."[15]

Destined for Greatness

While in London, Morse did two pieces of work that were so good they surprised many of the older artists. One was a great painting of the dying Hercules, a Greek **mythological** character. It was judged to be one of the 12 best works in an exhibit at the **Royal Academy**. There were 2,000 pictures in the exhibit!

> **mythological:** Lacking factual basis or historical validity

> **Royal Academy:** A society founded in 1768 by George III of England for the establishment of a school of design which held an annual exhibition of the works of living artists

The judges saw clearly that this was the work of a young man who was destined to make his mark in the art world. They would have been very surprised if they could have known that he would become world famous in an entirely different kind of activity: inventing.

A couple of years went by and Morse continued to draw and paint. He returned to America in 1832, hoping to earn money with his improved skills. He found that sometimes art paid very well and at other times it was hard to sell anything. Portraits sold better than some other paintings, so when times were hard he returned to portraits. He went to Europe again briefly in 1832. It was on the way home that the course of his life work took an unexpected turn.

He found his fellow passengers on the ship to be pleasant company. Many enjoyable conversations happened at the dinner table and on the deck. One day at dinner the conversation turned to experiments with electricity.

"I have heard," one man said, "that a current of electricity will pass along a very long wire almost instantly."

Another man replied that indeed, a current would pass along the longest wires in less than a second. "Dr. Franklin used wires several miles long," he explained, "and he could detect no difference in time between the touch at one end of the wire and the resulting spark at the other."

This made Morse think. He knew that electricity had already been used to send signals over a wire. Why could it not be used to send messages? What a blessing that would be! He had heard people in the southern American states complain about how long it took to send a letter to a friend in the north. Mail from the south could take as much as a month to reach New York City. In that much time, a friend in Georgia could be dead and buried before his New York friend heard that he had been sick. He remembered his first trip to London. How he had wished then that he could let his mother know right away that he had arrived safely. There must be a way.

Back in New York, Morse was met by his brothers, and he excitedly told them of his idea. They were surprised that he seemed to have forgotten his strong desire to paint great pictures. Now he seemed completely distracted by the idea of his new invention. His brothers supported and encouraged him to follow his new dream. He moved into a room in brother Richard's new home and began to experiment.

He had heard of experiments with **electromagnetism**. In this process, a round bar of metal was turned into a magnet by an electrified wire wrapped around it. Finley's idea was to link a pencil with an **electromagnet** to make a mark on paper when the electricity started to flow through the wire. The current could be interrupted to stop the magnetism and allow the pencil to lift off the paper. When the switch lever was just tapped for a split second, the pencil would leave a dot on the paper as it moved across rollers. If it was held down a little longer, it would make a line. Finley developed a code using dots and lines, which he called dashes. Dots and dashes. A new language, powered by the miracle of electricity, would soon carry messages across America in seconds! The more Finley worked on his project, the more firmly he believed that God had made electricity to be a blessing to man.

> **electromagnetism:** The branch of physics dealing with the interaction of electric currents
>
> **electromagnet:** A soft metal core made into a magnet by the passage of electric current through a coil surrounding it

Finally Good News

The next few years were difficult. Finley's work on the telegraph kept him away from painting and he became very poor. Morse was penniless and frequently hungry, but he never took his eyes off God. During this time, Morse wrote, "I am perfectly satisfied that, mysterious as it may seem to me, it has all been ordered in view of my Heavenly Father's guiding hand."[16]

Even though he developed models that showed clearly that his invention could work, it was hard to get wealthy people to invest their money in such a new and strange project. What if it failed and their money was never repaid? He approached the federal government. Would they vote to invest thousands of dollars in this new creation? Could he convince them that the telegraph would really make life in America better for everyone? At long last, in 1843, his request was put up for a vote in the Senate.

The last day of the Senate session came, and still his request had not been voted on. Many bills were to be put to a vote that day. As the hours wore on, Finley slowly lost hope that his request for funds would be passed. Late in the evening he gave up hope and went to his hotel room and to bed.

The next morning, he entered the hotel dining room for breakfast. A servant told him a young lady was waiting to see him. He was surprised to see that his visitor was young Annie Ellsworth, the daughter of his friend, H.L. Ellsworth. With a smile, Morse reached out a hand to her. "What brings you to see me so early in the day, my young friend?"

She replied that she had come to congratulate him on the passage of his bill in the Senate.

"No, you are mistaken," he said sadly. "I stayed in the chamber until the lamps were lighted and my friends assured me there was no chance for me."

"It is you who are mistaken," she insisted. "Father was there until they left at midnight and even saw the president sign the bill. This morning he told me I might come over and congratulate you."

For a moment Finley just stood and stared at the girl. He could hardly believe such good news. When he could speak, he said, "You were the first to bring me this welcome news, Annie, and I promise you that you shall send the first message over my telegraph when it is done."[17]

On May 24, 1844, the telegraph line from Washington, D.C. to Baltimore was finished. Finley Morse remembered his promise to Annie Ellsworth. He asked her what her first message should be. "What hath God wrought!" she replied, quoting a verse from the Bible. Morse was very pleased with her suggestion. He wanted to give God all the credit for leading him to success with his invention. Later he said, "It baptized the American telegraph with the name of its Author."[18]

In the years to come, messages would be flashed across America in seconds. Soon after that, they would cross from America to Europe in cables under the Atlantic. Indeed, it did seem a miracle that was far greater than the works of a man.

5

Louis Pasteur – The Boy Who Asked Questions

| 1822–1895 | French chemist and microbiologist |

Who Was Louis Pasteur?

Born in 1822 in Dole, France, Louis Pasteur was born to a poor family. Louis, even as a young boy, had a great desire to increase his knowledge. Louis longed to use the science he loved to benefit ordinary people. Louis Pasteur's personal life included sickness and tragedy. Three of his five children died of childhood diseases. His sister was left **intellectually disabled** by a childhood disease. These tragedies inspired him to try to find cures. Through all his trials, Pasteur was sustained by his Christian faith.

The Chemist's Shop

There weren't many shops in the little town of Arbois, France, in the early 1800s, but on the main street, there was a chemist's shop. The chemist was a very important man in the village. He sold pills and liquid mixtures and skin creams, just as druggists do today. In those days, the chemist had to do much more. He mixed up many of his medicines right in the shop. For some of them, he mixed chemical powders together. For other medicines, he prepared herbs that grew in the nearby fields and mountains. If you happened to come to the shop and find it closed, it might be because the chemist was out in the meadows looking for healing plants.

The chemist's shop was a fascinating place for one little Arbois boy. His name was Louis

> **intellectually:** Related to how a person's brain works
>
> **disabled:** A condition that limits or creates challenges for a person

Pasteur, and he was only five years old. Yet he would stand for hours beside the marble table on which the chemist mixed his medicines. Nearly every day Louis would visit the shop and watch as the life-giving mixtures were prepared. He loved to watch the man grind roots to powder or mix colored liquids and pour them into bottles. He watched as the man labeled each bottle and wrote upon it a mysterious Latin name.

Louis listened to the customers who came to the chemist for help. They told him about their problems or the problems of their farm animals. The chemist would listen thoughtfully to their symptoms. Then he might ask a few questions and listen to the answers. Usually, he would tell them to come back the next day for the medicines he would mix up to help them.

Little Louis did not talk much while in the shop. But he watched and listened to all that went on. Indeed, that was the way the boy acted wherever he was. He was a serious little boy who thought about things constantly. His family had moved to Arbois because two little sisters had been added to the Pasteur family and a larger house was needed. Also, Mr. Pasteur needed a house in a good location to work at his trade.

Louis' father was a tanner, a man who made leather out of animal skins. Tanning required a lot of water, so a tanner's shop needed to be near a river or creek. The Pasteurs found the perfect house on the banks of the Cuisance River in Arbois. In the cellar, Louis' father kept great bins of salt to be used in the tanning process. When the sheep and cattle skins arrived, he placed them in the bins and buried them in the salt.

"Why do you do that?" little Louis asked one day.

"To keep them from rotting," his father answered.

Louis had his deep-in-thought look on his face again. "How does salt keep them from rotting?" he wanted to know.

His father shrugged patiently. "I don't know. No one knows. Some say it's just the way things are, and we should not question it."

Louis asked, "Do other things spoil the same way?"

Mr. Pasteur smiled. He sometimes got tired of his son's endless questions, but he was glad they were asked. He was happy that his little boy was so bright and curious. He hoped one day to send Louis for a good education. Perhaps he would even become a teacher.

"A lot of things spoil, my son. Meat can spoil and make you sick. Milk can go sour one day even though it was sweet and fresh just the day before. Wine can become bitter, like some of Mr. DuPont's did last year. It's a shame, because wine and cheese are important things in France. Many people earn their living making them. Someday perhaps we will find a way to keep them from spoiling."

Someday

Louis thought about this. Something needed to be done to keep good food from being destroyed. In his young mind, a resolution began to form and grow. Someday he would be the man to find an answer. Someday he would help the dairy farmer and the vineyard owner. He would make a difference!

Finally, the day came for little Louis to start school. His mother packed his lunch bag and kissed him goodbye. His father walked with him to the school gate, then turned and walked home. Across the schoolyard, Louis spotted his best friend, Jules Vercel. "Jules!" he shouted and ran to join him. They selected seats next to each other in the classroom. School was going to be fun!

Louis was a serious student as well as a fun-loving boy. He wanted to do well in school so his parents would be proud. When he did addition and subtraction, his numbers were neat and in perfect rows. He took his time and made every letter he wrote look just right.

Trying to get work done perfectly takes time. Louis' teacher noticed that the boy was slow and thought that he wasn't a very bright student. One day he told Louis' parents that their son worked very hard and was well-behaved, but that he did not seem to have much ability for school. He seemed slow to learn.

His mother and father knew him better than the teacher did. They understood that their boy was just taking his time to do his work the very best he could. Each night, they read his lessons to him and asked him questions about them. Mrs. Pasteur bought him new pencils and encouraged him to draw pictures. Looking over her son's shoulder, she noticed that he looked at things carefully and thought long and hard before starting to draw. It was this carefulness that made him seem to be a slow student.

Every week he visited his friend, the chemist. He looked at all the minerals, roots, and herbs the man had gathered for making medicines. He asked questions about where they came from and how they would be used to cure sickness. He even made drawings of some of those things. He wanted to someday be able to help people who were sick.

Trouble Comes

He did not have long to wait. One day he and his friend, Jules, were fishing at a quiet spot on the Cuisance River. On that summer day in 1831, the quiet of the place was pierced by screams.

"Help! Help me! A wolf bit me!" It was Annette, the little girl who lived next door to Louis. Terrified, she was running toward them, crying. Dropping their fishing poles and running to her side, the boys saw blood dripping from bite marks on her leg.

Louis tried to calm her. "Don't worry, Annette," he urged. "We'll take you home."

When they reached the village, Jules took Annette to her house and Louis ran for the doctor. He was very frightened for Annette because he knew how deadly a bite from a wolf could be. Eight people in the town had already died after having been bitten by a wolf. The animal was sick with a virus called rabies. Many kinds of animals can get rabies and sometimes they go mad and bite other animals and people. In those days, people did not understand what causes rabies and they did not have good ways of treating it. It was a very dangerous disease.

Annette lived after her frightening wolf encounter, but most people did not. Louis wanted to know more about rabies. He asked the doctor, the chemist, and his teacher at school. No one knew the answers to his questions. He pondered the problem in his mind. What caused rabies? What could be done to prevent it? He realized he had met with another great health menace. Someone needed to find a solution.

Time went by and Louis grew up. He had changed in many ways, but he was still filled with curiosity and still a hard-working student. He became a university professor of physics at the **Dijon Lycée** in 1848, which made his parents very proud and happy. But even though his teaching changed the lives of his students, it was in the laboratory that he made the discoveries that changed the world. Here he explored the mysteries of creation and looked to the great Creator for answers to his perplexing questions. He once said, "The more I study nature, the more I stand amazed at the work of the Creator. I pray while I am engaged at my work in the laboratory."[19]

Dijon Lycée: A secondary school attended before college

The Answer

He worked long, hard hours after teaching his classes. He used every tool the university laboratory offered. He created tests and ran them over and over. He kept detailed records of every test. He searched for clues to questions that could mean life or death for millions of people. And he found answers.

He learned about microscopic creatures called bacteria. Here were the tiny culprits for which he had been searching for years! It was bacteria that caused milk to spoil. Bacteria caused meat to rot. Bacteria were the deadly little villains that caused human disease. Peering through the lens of his microscope hour after hour, day after day, Louis Pasteur began to unravel the mystery of bacteria.

Studying milk was a way to clearly show the relationship between bacteria and the spoiling process. Little was known about this in the mid-1800s, but Louis could prove it to anyone who cared to look through his microscope. Looking at a drop of fresh milk under the microscope, few bacteria were seen. When the slide contained spoiled milk, they were there by the thousands. The same was true with other liquids.

Then Louis discovered that heating milk kept it fresh and free of bacteria much longer than milk that had not been heated. The heat seemed to kill the bacteria. This process of heating milk to kill germs made Louis world-famous. It came to be called pasteurization. Nearly all the milk that we drink today is pasteurized.

This was just one of many great discoveries that the quiet boy from Arbois gave to the world. He also developed a vaccine to prevent rabies. Another of his vaccines cured anthrax, a deadly disease that can kill farm animals and even people. Pasteur's findings helped established a new branch of science — **microbiology**. These are just a few of the many ways the poor tanner's son made the world a better, healthier place.

microbiology: The branch of science that deals with microorganisms

Alexander Graham Bell and the Talking Machine

| 1847–1922 | Born in Scotland, then relocated to the United States |

Who was Alexander Graham Bell?

Alexander Graham Bell was a Scottish-born inventor, scientist, and engineer who is credited with patenting the first practical telephone. Alexander was homeschooled by his mother, who instilled in him an infinite curiosity about the world around him. He and his family moved to Canada in 1870 and then a year later settled in Boston, Massachusetts. He is credited with more than 18 patents for his inventions.

He invented the telephone, but he would not have one in his office. Alexander Bell had been inventing things long before he made the first effective telephone, and he wanted to keep on inventing and discovering. For that reason, he kept his home telephone at a distance when he was working. He did not have time to be interrupted by calls when he was hot on the trail of a new discovery.

Fascinated by Sound

Sound had always been interesting and important to Alexander. Born in Scotland in 1847, Alexander was the son and the grandson of men who made their living teaching people how to speak correctly. They were called **elocutionists** and their science was **elocution**. Sometimes they worked with deaf people, teaching them to read lips to understand others and to speak, even though they could not hear their own words. This allowed others to be able to understand them.

elocutionist: A public speaker trained in voice production/oratory

elocution: The skill of clear and articulate speech

Alexander's father would sometimes do demonstrations for the public. Alexander would help him show how he taught deaf people to understand words and then to say them. But the main reason for young Alexander's great interest in words and sound was his mother. When Aleck, as he was called by his family and friends, was 12, his mother began to lose her hearing. Aleck found that if he spoke in a clear, calm voice with his lips very close to her forehead, his mother could understand him. This made him wonder about sound and how it traveled.

Aleck wondered about many things. He loved to explore and experiment. He and his brothers had a little museum in which they displayed wildflowers, bones, and bugs they found in their wanderings.

Music was also important to the Bell family. Mrs. Bell played the piano, and the family sang together nearly every evening. As years went by and his mother's hearing grew weaker and weaker, Aleck told himself that someday he would invent ways to help deaf people hear again. Everyone needed to be able to communicate with friends and family.

A Talking Machine

One day in 1863, Mr. Bell came home from a trip. As his wife and children asked him for an account of his travels, he said that the most interesting thing he had seen was a talking machine. Aleck and his brother, Melville, were almost shaking with eagerness. They begged their father to tell them how the wonderful machine worked.

"I don't think I'll tell you how it worked," he said thoughtfully. "It didn't talk very well. I'll bet you boys could make a better talking machine if you put your minds to it. After all, you know more than most boys about speech and how it is made."[20]

This was true. Their father had taught them much about his work. He had figured out a way to teach people to make words and sounds. Mr. Bell called his system "Visible Speech." It had ten signs that meant a certain way of placing the tongue and lips so that a person could follow the signs to make the right sounds. Melville and Aleck also knew that speech was made by the lungs, tongue, lips, and vocal cords. They decided to try to make their own talking machine.

They gathered the things they thought they would need and started in eagerly. They wanted a machine that looked something like a real person instead of just a box that talked. It would have a head, mouth, throat, and lungs. A tongue made of rubber and stuffed with cotton was placed inside the head. Lips were made of wire, then covered with rubber. They made vocal cords out of thin metal. The lungs were **bellows** like the ones used to blow on a fire to make it burn hotter.

When the machine was finally ready, the brothers showed the family how it worked. Melville pumped the bellows to send air through the vocal cords. Aleck moved the lips and tongue to form a word. "Mama! Mama!" the machine said.[21] Mr. Bell looked with pride at his boys.

bellows: A device with an airbag that blows a stream of air when squeezed

"This is a better talking machine than the one I saw in London!" he said happily.[22]

Sometimes, Aleck's desire to learn for himself caused problems. After receiving his early education at home, he went to school for a few years. School was hard for him because he did not like being told things and then writing reports on them. He loved to discover things for himself.

However, he did make good grades in science classes. Science was interesting to the boy, and he especially liked biology. There was a mystery about plants and animals that Aleck loved. His other classes were less interesting to him and he was often absent. He left school at 15 and did not go back until it was time for college.

After leaving school, Aleck went to London and stayed a year with his grandfather. Here Aleck found that learning could be fun. He spent long hours in serious study and discussion with his grandfather. Grandfather Bell wanted his pupil to learn to speak clearly and with conviction. He hoped that his grandson would one day be a teacher too.

In 1868 Aleck was enrolled in the University of London. He paid for part of his school expenses by teaching music classes. He began experimenting in many ways with sound and electricity. Then both his brothers died from tuberculosis. Aleck himself became very sick. His father decided to move the family to Canada in 1870, hoping that the climate would make him healthy again. There they bought a small farm and Aleck cleaned out the old carriage house to make himself a workshop. His experiments continued.

School for the Deaf

In less than a year, Aleck's health had improved greatly. He wanted to go back to teaching. A new school for deaf children had opened in Boston and Aleck was offered a job teaching there. The school wanted him to use his father's Visible Speech method to help the deaf children to speak. Once school started, Aleck began giving private speech lessons as well. His first student was a six-year-old boy named George Sanders. Using Visible Speech, Aleck taught George to speak. Of course, this made George's parents very happy!

Another private student was a pretty 15-year-old young lady named Mabel Hubbard. Mabel had lost her hearing at age 4. She was very bright and had learned to read and write although she could not hear. She could also read lips, so she understood what other people were saying. She could talk, but her father wanted her to learn to speak much more clearly. So Mr. Hubbard brought Mabel to Aleck for Visible Speech lessons.

Mabel's father liked Aleck and was interested in his inventions. He began inviting Aleck to his home and soon the Hubbards and Alexander Graham Bell were close friends. Mr. Hubbard was a wealthy lawyer. His daughter's hearing problem had made him interested in helping schools for deaf children. He was pleased with the work Aleck had done with Mabel and wanted more children to be able to have such wonderful help. He and Aleck spent many hours talking about sound and Aleck's inventions.

The telegraph had been invented, making it possible to send messages across America in just seconds. Before that time, the Pony Express had been the fastest way to send messages. But the pony riders took several days to carry the mail across the country, braving robbers, Native Americans, and bad weather along their difficult route. Now the telegraph had opened a new world of possibilities by using electricity to carry news through the wires. Aleck was fascinated by the telegraph. He wanted to invent ways to improve it.

The biggest problem was money. It took money to buy the materials needed for his experiments. Mr. Hubbard and Mr. Sanders agreed to help Aleck because they liked the teaching he had given their children. Soon Aleck was looking for help with his work.

Mr. Watson

Aleck was good at coming up with ideas about how to make new things. But he was not as good at making them. Aleck paid a machine shop to make the things he needed. A man in the shop named Thomas Watson seemed to be an excellent mechanic, so Aleck asked him to work with him on his idea for a new and better type of telegraph.

Aleck and Mabel Hubbard had grown very fond of each other by now, but Aleck had little time to spend with her. After their work at school and in the machine shop, Aleck and Thomas worked at night on their project. Some nights they were so excited about it that they did not go to sleep at all. Then Aleck had a new idea. Why not make a machine that would allow people to talk over wires, rather than just send messages?

He and Watson talked about it. They knew that sound is made by vibrations passing through air. What if sound waves could also travel by an electrical current? They went to work on the new machine.

Months went by as they experimented. They built new kinds of **transmitters** to send the message. They built new kinds of receivers to receive the message. They tried new ways of connecting wires. Still, they could not find a way to send sound from a transmitter to a receiver.

> **transmitters:** Equipment used to generate and send messages

Then one night Aleck and Watson were working in different rooms in the shop. Aleck was working on the receiver while Watson was working on the transmitter. Suddenly, Aleck heard a noise. It seemed to come through the receiver! Rushing into the other room, Aleck asked, "What did you just do?"[23]

Watson said that the transmitter had jammed and that he had been trying to fix it. When he moved the part that was stuck, it made a "twang" sound. Almost holding their breath, the two men tried sending the sound over and over again. It worked! Now they knew it was possible to send sound over wires.

Now the two friends worked harder than ever. They took time away from the telegraph project. Aleck stopped teaching for a while. Day and night they worked on the talking machine. On March 10, 1876, they were hard at work. Watson was working on the receiver downstairs. Upstairs, Aleck was working on the transmitter. His workbench was covered with wires, tools, battery acid, and other materials. Suddenly, Aleck bumped the acid container and acid spilled out on his clothes.

He cried out, "Mr. Watson, come here! I want to see you." Then he remembered that Thomas Watson was too far away to hear him.

But to his surprise, Watson came bounding up the stairs. "Mr. Bell, I heard you!" he said, panting. "I heard every word!"[24]

Suddenly the acid burns were forgotten. Alexander Graham Bell and Thomas Watson spent the rest of the night talking on their new machine. At last, it had worked. They called it the "telephone."

Years went by. Aleck and Mabel got married and had two daughters. It took a long time for people to see how valuable the telephone was, but finally, Mr. Saunders and Mr. Hubbard helped Aleck start the Bell Telephone Company. More and more people got telephones in their homes. Aleck's invention changed the way people all over the world live their lives.

But he could not stop inventing and discovering. He had too many ideas! He made an instrument to help doctors find metal objects in a human body. He studied flight and experimented with gliders and kites. He explored ways to change ocean salt water into drinking water. He predicted that people would fly someday. People laughed at the idea, but Aleck insisted it was true. People had once laughed at his telephone idea, too.

Alexander Graham Bell became one of the world's most famous men. Newspaper articles were written about him. Famous people came to meet him. His name was known around the world. His invention was one of the greatest in history.

Yet, for the rest of his life, he would say that his most important work had been as a "teacher of the deaf."

7

Thomas Edison – Just the Strange Boy the World Needed

| 1847–1931 | American inventor and businessman |

Who Was Thomas Edison?

What would you think of a boy who sat on goose eggs, trying to hatch them? What would you think if you knew that that same boy would only go to school for three months in his entire life? Would you expect that boy to grow up to be the greatest inventor of all time, known all over the world as a **genius**? You probably would not. Yet, that is what happened in the life of that boy. His name was Thomas Edison.

Growing Up Years

Edison was known by his middle name, Alva. Some of his friends and family called him Al. He was born on February 11, 1847. His father was a hard-working man who earned his living making wood shingles for house roofs.

The Edison home was a **modest** house on a bluff overlooking the Huron River and the canal beside it. In those days there were no great highways and huge trucks to haul goods across the country. So, the rivers and canals moved things on boats from one place to another. This made the little town of Milan, Ohio, a wonderful place to grow up. There were so many people and so many wagons and boats coming and going. A child never knew what interesting person he or she might meet or what amazing thing might happen as he or she wandered around Milan.

In harvest time, the little village rumbled with the noise of heavy farm wagons bringing grain to be hauled away on the canal boats. Farmers from far and near brought their crops to be carried down the canal to Lake Erie. Teams of four or six horses pulled the heavy wagons along

> **genius:** Exceptional intellectual ability
>
> **modest:** Humble

dusty roads, sweating in their harnesses. Sometimes as many as 600 wagons creaked along through the town in a single day! Little Al came to know many men and boys who came with the wagons. Of course, he also knew many of the people who lived in Milan all the time.

Al was the kind of boy who could not sit at home and do nothing, for his restless mind drove him to look and listen and learn from everything around him. He would never spend much time in school, but he loved learning and found it everywhere. When he was a small child and had not yet learned to read and write, an old man noticed little Al sitting on the ground in front of the village store. He was holding a board on his lap, trying to copy the letters on the store's sign with chalk!

School did not work out well for Thomas Alva Edison. After only three months of schooling, Al's teacher told Mrs. Edison that the boy's mind did not work well. He was asking too many questions. At that, Al's mother turned red in the face and told the teacher that asking questions was the best thing a child could do if he really wanted to learn. Al did not go back to that school or any other. His mother began to teach him at home on the front porch. She called it "exploring" the wonderful world of learning. Young Al loved it.

His mother was a delightful teacher, making lessons fun. But lessons at home did not take nearly all day, as school had done. This left Al with plenty of time to wander around town, talking with the other boys and the farmers and boatmen who did business in Milan. He found that he could learn from everyone he met. He was full of questions and impatient to know the answer whenever a question came to his mind.

Business

In Edison's day, children did not have to go to school for many years as most of them do now. When Al was 12 years old, his father gave him permission to look for a job and start earning money for himself. The boy found a place working for the Grand Trunk Railroad selling newspapers and candy to the passengers. It was a fitting job for such a boy. Al was friendly and smart. He had a **jovial** forward manner that made the passengers like him. He seemed to know just the thing to say to amuse the people and make them want what he was selling.

jovial: Cheerful and friendly

He soon learned that newspaper sales went up or down, depending on what news they carried. Some stories were more interesting to the train riders and people in the towns where the train stopped than other stories. Al would scan the papers carefully, judging just how many he could sell on that day. This was during the Civil War and there was often exciting news of great battles. When that happened, Al knew there would be a big demand for papers on the train. One day there was news about the battle of Pittsburgh Landing. Al thought, "I could sell a thousand of these papers if I had them, and if people already knew that there had been a big battle."[25]

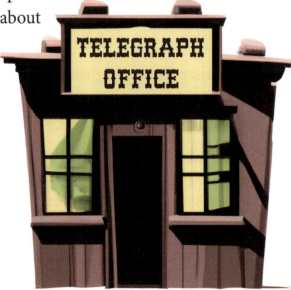

Thomas Alva Edison was not the boy to see an opportunity and let it go by. He set his creative mind to work at once. Running to the telegraph office at the first stop, he begged the telegraph operator to send the news of the battle down the line. Soon the wires were carrying the tidings that a great conflict had taken place. As this news reached towns and villages, people began telling others that something important would be in the newspapers when the train brought them. The anticipation began to spread.

Now how was he to get a thousand copies of the newspaper without money? This problem would have made many a young person give up the idea, but not Thomas Edison. He ran to the office of the Detroit Free Press. He asked the business manager to give him one thousand copies on credit. The man refused. What an **upstart** this bold boy was! But Al persevered. He appeared at the office of the newspaper's editor, Mr. Story.

upstart: Not afraid to try new things

"I need a thousand copies of your paper with the story of the battle," he told the editor. "I have no money to pay for them, but I will sell them quickly and bring you the money then."[26]

Mr. Story looked down at the confident youngster and liked what he saw. "How would you find buyers for so many papers?" he asked.

Without hesitating, Al told him what he had done to arouse interest in people all down the railroad line. Mr. Story smiled and gave him an order for a thousand copies.

Not only did the telegraph message sell papers; it sold them beyond Al's fondest hopes. Grand Trunk passengers snatched them eagerly as Al went from car to car, shouting that he had news of the latest great battle. When the train rolled into the stations, townspeople were already crowding the platforms crying for the news. There was so much demand that Al raised his price first to 10 cents and later to 25 cents. In one day's work, he made so much profit that he felt he had earned a fortune.

Al's work on the train helped him to make the best use of his natural curiosity, as he daily saw many different places and met many people. He thought nearly everything that happened was interesting and he paid attention to all that was going on around him. He was full of questions and full of ideas for interesting projects. Some of his projects earned money for him, but he was just as happy if they only helped answer his questions.

His dealing with the newspaper office had made friends for him there. He got some **type** from the Detroit Free Press and started his own newspaper, printing it on the train and filling it with news that was interesting to the people who worked and rode on the Grand Trunk. He also set up his laboratory in the same baggage car and did chemical experiments. At the public library in Detroit, he set about to read as many books as time allowed. Eventually, he read all the books on a shelf 15 feet long. But he did not stop there. By then he had found that some books contained much more useful information than other books, so from that time on he chose his books more carefully. And he went on reading.

> **type:** Physical letters used to make words for a newspaper to be printed from

All the time, Al kept learning also from the experience of working on the train. But there were some setbacks as well. One day, the jolting of the train rattled the bottles and boxes on his laboratory shelves. A bottle of **phosphorous** fell to the floor and broke. Suddenly, smoke began to fill the baggage car. The wooden floor was on fire! The flames

> **phosphorous:** A poisonous, combustible substance that ignites easily in the air

were extinguished quickly, but the conductor had had his fill of chemicals on his train. He threw out Al's entire laboratory. He was so angry and frantic that he even threw out the printing press too! Fortunately, Al did not lose his job, but he gave up the publishing business and moved his laboratory to his father's cellar.

This was the childhood of the world's greatest inventor. All of life was an education to Thomas Alva Edison and he was determined to make the most of it. While still a boy, he really did try sitting on goose eggs, attempting to hatch them. He and a neighbor boy ran a telegraph line two miles so they could send messages between their homes. Once he mixed up a concoction to make a person lighter than air so he could fly. The boy he persuaded to drink the mixture did not get the power to fly; he only got a belly ache. Al got a spanking.

From Boyhood to Manhood

So young Thomas Edison explored the world around him. Questioning, searching, reading, trying, succeeding, failing. Day by day, experiment by experiment, the boy grew into the man who would one day light up the world.

When we read about history, we often see the names of people who accomplished amazing things. They were important people, people whose lives affected the lives of many other people. Some of our historical heroes were important because they fought and won wars. Others were important because they held high offices in government, such as presidents and kings. Still others found their way into history books because they discovered or invented things that changed the way most people live their lives.

Thomas Edison was one of these people. He was the most successful inventor in American history, if we use the number of his inventions and discoveries as the method of comparison. In a 60-year career, Edison obtained 1,093 patents from the United States Patent Office. He also was granted over 2,000 patents by other nations.

Edison indeed changed the world. He was the first person to create a successful light bulb. Others had known that electricity could be used to produce light, but no one had made a light bulb that would shine brightly and last a long time before burning out. Edison experimented for years with hundreds of different materials and would not give up until he succeeded. Because of his determination, America left the old way of lighting homes and businesses with kerosene lamps and moved into a new era.

But the electric light was just one of Edison's many inventions. He made the first phonograph, which came to be called the record player. He invented the movie camera. He advanced X-ray technology. The list of things Edison invented or improved goes on and on. We all owe much to Thomas Edison because our lives are easier and healthier thanks to his brilliance and hard work. The boy the schoolteachers didn't want became one of the world's great geniuses.

8

Booker T. Washington – From Slavery to Triumph

| 1856–1915 | A slave in Virginia to President of Tuskegee Institute in Alabama |

Who was Booker T. Washington?

Booker T. Washington was an inspiration, having risen from being a young slave to college president. Two things he taught to others were the benefits of hard work and a reliance on the Word of God. He rejoiced that he and his students at the Tuskegee Institute had to endure hard times. He noted repeatedly that it is in those hard times when we learn the greatest lessons. Rather than an easy road, he preferred to tackle problems, knowing the struggle itself would make him a better man.

He once said, "You never read in history of any great man whose influence has been lasting, who has not been a reader of the Bible."[27]

Longing to Learn

Little Booker looked up from his hoeing and took a moment to get his breath. The Virginia sky was a hazy blue above him, stretching from woods to woods on all sides. It had been cool early this morning when he had carried Miss Ellen's books to school for her. He had lingered at the school for a moment after Miss Ellen had gone in and the schoolmaster had started taking attendance. Looking in the open window, he felt a deep longing as he saw the students getting settled for a day of study. Oh, how he wished he could be in that little building, learning to read and write! Somehow he understood that there was a whole new world within the pages of those books. Someday, he must find a way to learn.

Life as a Slave

But now it was late morning and the southern sun was blazing overhead. Booker looked around, leaning on his hoe. His owner, Mr. Burroughs and his sons had worked in the fields along with their slaves until the war came. The Burroughs farm was not a wealthy one and everybody had to work. But Mr. James, the owner of the farm, had died and his sons had gone off to fight in the southern army during the Civil War. Already the news had come that one of the Burroughs's sons had been killed in battle. Now the old farm was a sad place and the Burroughs women were struggling to keep the place going.

Booker's mother, Jane, was the cook on the plantation and all her children worked at whatever jobs they were able to do. The little cabin that was their home was rough — hot in the summer and cold in the winter. Their beds were ragged quilts on the dirt floor. They ate a simple and **scanty** diet. Booker's only clothing was a long shirt made of rough material.

He went back to his hoeing. Chop, chop, chop, was heard as the little weeds fell and he loosened the soil around the corn roots. The sun was hot on his bare head. Someday, he would learn something more interesting than farm work. Someday, he would learn to read. Someday, he would make something of his life.

scanty: Very, very little

Days and years went by before Booker saw the beginning of his path to a better life. Then one day a Yankee soldier came to the farm to talk to the Burroughs family. Booker had heard the slave gossip that the war had been lost and the Burroughs boys would soon be coming home. News traveled quickly from farm to farm through the slave communication network. Now he knew it was true. The war was over. Was it also true that he and his family would be free? He had heard that rumor as well, but it had almost seemed too good to be true.

All the slaves were called to the Burrough's big house. They quickly assembled in the yard, whispering among themselves. They felt that some great announcement was to be made, but hardly dared to believe that freedom had come to them. Some of them held their breath as the soldier in blue stepped out on the front porch. In his hand, he held a sheet of paper. Looking around at the faces before him, he began to read.

Forever Free

Eight-year-old Booker did not understand all the big words as they were read, but he heard gasps from the adults around him as the soldier spoke the phrase, "thenceforth and forever free." For a moment the people stood in shocked silence. They could hardly believe what they had heard. Then Jane bent over and whispered to Booker and his siblings, "Now, my children, we are free!"

That was the beginning of a new chapter for Booker and all the workers on the Burroughs farm. It was exciting — amazing — that they could go anywhere they wanted to go and take any job they could get. But it was frightening, too. All their lives they had not had to make such decisions. Now they would make the decisions for themselves. They would have to find a way to work to have food, a place to live, but at long last, they were not slaves any more! In the end, most of the older slaves worked out an agreement with the Burroughs family to stay and work as freed employees.

Jane wanted to take her children to a different place for a new start in life. Her husband, Booker's stepfather, was already free and living in Malden, West Virginia. Now she could take her children there and they could live as a real family together. She had hundreds of miles to travel and very little money, but she was determined to go.

When they reached Malden, Booker's ears pricked up as he heard that there was a school for black children there. But his family was very poor and he had to take a job in the salt mine where his stepfather worked to help support them. There was very little time for learning when the hard work of packing salt in barrels started at 4 a.m.

Booker was hungry to learn. Somehow he got his hands on a spelling book. His mother asked the schoolmaster to teach her son for a little while each day after work. Booker's little world was growing larger.

After a time in the salt mine, Booker found a better job in a coal mine. The work was hard, dirty, and dangerous. But the pay was a little better. Then one day he heard two of the workers talking about a new school for African Americans or former slaves. It was called Hampton College, and students did not have to have any money to learn there! They could pay for their schooling by working around the school. Booker's heart leaped. Hampton was the place for him.

Hampton at Last

Finally, when Booker was 16, his parents said he could go to Hampton. They would find a way to get by without his pay from the coal mine. No sacrifice was too great if it would help their son get an education. They did not have much money to pay for his 500-mile trip, but others stepped in to help. The former slaves in the community were nearly as excited as Booker was. One of their own was going to college! Gladly they collected their pennies to help him get there.

It was a hard trip. Often Booker had to walk. Sometimes, kindly people gave him a ride in their wagon or buggy when he met them along the road. After two weeks of travel, Booker found himself in Richmond. Hampton College in Hampton, Virginia, was only 80 miles away now. But he had used up all his money. Where could he sleep? How could he get food? He went to the hotel and offered to work in exchange for food and a room. He was turned away.

The city was very strange to Booker, the country boy. It was busy and noisy and did not seem friendly to a boy traveling alone. After trudging around Richmond for a long time he finally found a space underneath a **boardwalk** where he could sleep. He was very tired, but until late that night he could not fall asleep. Footsteps on the boardwalk above him boomed loud in the night.

> **boardwalk:** A walkway across sand or marshy ground, usually made of wood

The next morning, Booker crawled out from his hiding place and went looking for work. Down at the docks by the river was a big ship being unloaded. Booker asked the man in charge if he needed any help with the unloading. He gave Booker work for a few days and then the young student was on his way again. With his wages jingling in his pocket, he started the final stage of his journey to Hampton Institute.

At long, long last Booker stood looking up at the high brick walls of Hampton. Here was where he would spend the next few years of his life. Here was where he would make something of himself. First, though, he had to get past Miss Mackie.

Miss Mackie was the head teacher of the school. She would decide whether Booker would be accepted as a student. As she stood looking at Booker, he did not look like a scholar. He had just traveled 500 miles, mostly walking. He had not had a bath or a change of clothes for a week. He had slept for a few nights under a boardwalk. He was dirty and his clothes were ragged and rumpled. But she would give him a chance to prove himself.

The Broom Test

She gave Booker a broom and some cleaning cloths. She took him to a classroom, one which had not been used lately and needed cleaning. "Clean up this room," she told him, and left.

Booker did not intend to fail his first test at Hampton. To fail would mean it was also his last test there. He jumped into his work, determined to make that dusty room cleaner than it had ever been. He dusted the room and then swept it. Then he dusted it and swept it again. Then he did it a third time. He searched the room for any little cranny where dirt might have collected, rubbing and scrubbing until the room seemed to shine. Then he went to find Miss Mackie.

When she came back into the classroom, Miss Mackie stood still for a moment. Looking around, she seemed surprised. She walked around the room. Finally, she took out a white handkerchief and rubbed it along the top of the door frame. It came away still white as snow.

She looked down at Booker. "I guess you will do to enter this institution," she said. Booker's heart leaped within him. He was going to be a student at Hampton!

Booker T. Washington — From Slavery to Triumph

However, he would be more than a student. He had learned how to work hard in the coal mine. He had been driven to walk 500 miles by his hunger to learn. He threw himself into his studies and graduated with high honors. Then he went back to Malden to share what he had learned with his black friends there. For two years he taught children all day and then taught adults at night. Then Hampton called to him again. They wanted him to come back and be a teacher!

Tuskegee

Then one day a letter came to Hampton asking for information. General Armstrong, the head of the college, was asked for the name of a teacher who could go to Tuskegee in Alabama and start a new school for African Americans. He replied that Booker T. Washington was the man for the job. Booker was still in his first year of teaching at Hampton College, but with General Armstrong's encouragement, he agreed to go to Alabama. There at Tuskegee, he would become world famous.

The school that he had been hired to teach in was no more than a little, broken-down shanty. There were no desks, no blackboard, no books or pencils or paper. The group that was starting the school had collected enough money to pay a teacher for the first year, but that was all. Booker would have to raise the money himself for the little group of 30 students who came. The first few years would be very hard indeed.

Booker was determined, and he succeeded. He put the students to work, taking off his coat and setting the example himself.

Together they cleared land to grow their own food. They learned how to make bricks and build their own buildings. They spent part of their time in the classroom and part of it in creating their own school. He taught them that there is honor in doing honest work, even very humble work. The students began to take pride in their new school.

The news of an exciting new school began to spread. Soon Booker began getting invitations to speak to groups who thought they might like to give money to help the school grow. He proved to be a powerful speaker who could make audiences laugh or cry or give money.

Soon Booker's name was known across America. He was the man who was creating opportunities for the African American people of the South to overcome illiteracy and poverty to lead successful lives as free people. He continued to build Tuskegee Institute and the enrollment continued to grow. He hired more teachers and built more buildings. He even brought the famous scientist, George Washington Carver, to teach at Tuskegee. By the time Booker died in 1915, Tuskegee had grown into a magnificent university. It had over 100 well-equipped buildings and 1,500 students. There were 200 teachers coaching students in 38 different trades and professions.

For 35 years Booker T. Washington was among the most important leaders of African Americans in America. He was a friend and advisor to Presidents. He was a hero to millions.

> "While a great deal of stress is laid upon the industrial side of the work at Tuskegee, we do not neglect or overlook in any degree the religious and spiritual side. The school is strictly undenominational, but it is thoroughly Christian, and the spiritual training of the students is not neglected. Our preaching service, prayer meetings,

Sunday school, Christian Endeavour Society, Young Men's Christian Association, and various missionary organizations, testify to this." [28]

He also had good words to say about his fellow Christians:

"In my efforts to get money, I have often been surprised at the patience and deep interest of the ministers, who are besieged [pressed upon to help] on every hand and at all hours of the day for help. If no other consideration had convinced me of the value of the Christian life, the Christ-like work which the Church of all denominations in America has done during the last thirty-five years for the elevation [to rise above expected levels] of the black man would have made me a Christian." [29]

9

George Washington Carver — God's Plant Doctor

| 1864–1943 | American agricultural scientist and inventor |

Who Was George Washington Carver?

George Washington Carver was one of the most famous scientists of the 20th century. He was recognized all around the world as a genius. He was an artist, a musician, a teacher, and a **botanist**. He was honored in many ways while he was living and after he died. Statues of him were erected. His face was on postage stamps and coins. He was the first African American to receive a master's degree in college. Parks, schools, and ships were named after him.

> **botanist:** A plant expert

Born a Slave

Starting out in life, George had great problems to overcome. He was so sickly that his doctor did not expect him to live to be 21 years old. His father died and his mother was taken away from him when he was a baby. He was a slave.

George's parents were named Giles and Mary. They were bought by Moses Carver in 1855 and taken to his farm near Diamond, Missouri. Giles died before George was born. When George was a baby, kidnappers from Arkansas rode up to the Carver farm at night and stole George and his mother. They took them south to sell them.

Mr. Carver sent some men to find them and bring them back. Mary could not be found, but her baby boy was returned to the Carver home. He and his brother James were raised by Moses and Susan Carver as their own sons.

James was a healthy, strong boy. He learned to work with Mr. Carver in the fields. Little, sickly George was not strong enough for farm work, so "Aunt Susan" as he called Mrs. Carver, taught him to help with the housework. He learned to cook, clean, and do laundry. These skills would someday help him work his way through college. Many years later, he would teach young people that honest hard work was a good thing, even if that work was humble. He would say, "Learn to do common things uncommonly well; we must always keep in mind that anything that helps fill the dinner pail is valuable."[30]

Aunt Susan taught George to read and write. She and her husband encouraged him to learn all he could so that he would be prepared to help others in the future. Though he could not go to school in his early years because he was black, he was studying nature around his home. He loved to roam the woods and fields. He collected unusual rocks and observed the many wild plants and flowers. He later said that God spoke to him through the wild things he loved and that natural things would reveal their secrets to those who loved them. "All flowers talk to me and so do hundreds of little living things in the woods. I learn what I know by watching and loving everything.… Whatever you love opens its secrets to you," he would later say.[31]

George wanted to go to school and keep on learning. African American children were not allowed in the public school in **Diamond Grove**. So he made up his mind to move ten miles south to Neosho where there was a school for black children. With the permission of Mr. Carver and Aunt Susan, George one day set off walking down the road toward his first schooling.

Diamond Grove: Diamond is located on Diamond Grove Prairie, Missouri

When he reached Neosho it was late in the day and the school was closed. George hunted for a place to sleep and curled up on the hay in a barn.

George Washington Carver — God's Plant Doctor

Off to School

The next morning, George went looking for a place to live while he went to school. He met a kind black lady named Mariah Watkins who said she had a room in her home that he could use. He could pay for his room and board by working around the house and farm. When she asked his name, young George replied, "Carver's George." That was the name he had been known by all his life. Mrs. Watkins was not satisfied with that. She said she would call him George Carver. She encouraged him to study hard, which is exactly what he wanted to do. She encouraged him to learn all he could, then to go back out into the world and give his learning back to his people. This made a great impression on him.

George had learned many useful things from Aunt Susan, and now he learned more from Aunt Mariah (so called because she treated him with such kindness and care). Aunt Mariah was a nurse and midwife. She knew many natural remedies for illness and young George was eager to learn. While he was going to school and working for Aunt Mariah, he was also learning more about nature and the good things God had built into the world around us. The more he learned, the more he wanted to know.

It was not long before George had learned all he thought he could learn in the little school at Neosho. So he went west to Kansas, walking and hitching rides in wagons with other people who were moving. He was still a young teenager, but already he had learned many practical skills which he could use to earn a living while going to school.

Life was hard for George, but his faith in God kept him going.

George told later how his life as a Christian had begun:

> "I was just a mere boy when converted, hardly ten years old. There isn't much of a story to it. God just came into my heart one afternoon while I was alone in the "loft" of our big barn while I was shelling corn to carry to the mill to be ground into meal.
>
> A dear little white boy, one of our neighbors, about my age, came by one Saturday morning, and in talking and playing he told me he was going to Sunday school tomorrow morning. I was eager to know what a Sunday school was. He said they sang hymns and prayed. I asked him what prayer was and what they said. I do not remember what he said; only remember that as soon as he left I climbed up into the "loft," knelt down by the barrel of corn and prayed as best I could. I do not remember what I said. I only recall that I felt so good that I prayed several times before I quit.
>
> My brother and myself were the only colored children in that neighborhood and of course, we could not go to church or Sunday school, or school of any kind.
>
> That was my simple conversion, and I have tried to keep the faith."[32]

All his life, George would speak of how God helped him in his research and revealed the secrets of nature to him.

The Plant Doctor

Even as a young boy, he found that God was willing to teach him as he studied creation around him. He learned how to take care of many different kinds of plants. Often, he could cure a plant that was not healthy. Neighbors began calling him "The Plant Doctor."

Always, George wanted to learn more. Traveling many miles, he attended several different schools. He lived with foster families, helping around the houses and farms to pay for his room and board. In Minneapolis, Kansas, he attended high school. He worked as a cook to pay for his schooling. While in Minneapolis, George found that there was another George Carver in town. Sometimes he received the other George Carver's mail by mistake. So, he added a middle initial to his name to stop the confusion. It did not stand for a middle name, but it stopped the problem with mail. When a friend suggested that the initial W could stand for Washington, George decided it was a good idea. For the rest of his life, he was George Washington Carver.

George felt that God wanted him to go even further in his education, so he began applying to be admitted to different colleges. He had made very good grades, so he was accepted at Highland College in Highland, Kansas. Once more, he was on the road to the next school.

When he went to see the president of Highland College, he got a nasty surprise. He could not attend that college after all. Highland only accepted white students! The president told him that if he had known George's race, his application never would have been accepted. Poor George was once again rejected because he was black.

However, the young man believed God wanted him to get more education and to use his learning to help people. So after working at several jobs to save money, he once again began searching for a college. This time, he would make sure that the school he chose would welcome him before going.

In 1890, George began studying art and piano at Simpson College in Iowa. His art teacher, Etta Budd, quickly saw that he had an amazing talent for painting pictures of flowers and plants. He told her that he loved those things and was eager to learn more about them. She told George that he should study botany at the Iowa State Agricultural College in Ames, Iowa. Soon he was moving to a new school once again.

At Iowa State, George was the first African American student to attend the school. He worked hard at doing laundry for other students to pay his school bills. He also worked hard at his studies. He quickly showed the teachers that he was a very special young man. He learned very quickly what he was taught. But he went beyond the teachers and the textbooks to learn for himself. Again, God showed him things in his studies that others had not seen. When he graduated from college, the professors asked him to stay at Iowa State for two more years and earn his master's degree. He decided to do so.

One program of the college was the Experiment Station. It was created to do research projects that would use science to help the people of Iowa. There George studied under Professor Louis Pammel for two years. He did research on plant diseases. By the time he had earned his degree, his work had attracted considerable attention. The former slave became known across America as a nationally respected botanist.

Now a Teacher

Carver graduated again, this time with a master's degree. Still, he did not leave the school. His work had been so amazing that the school asked him to stay on as a teacher. George agreed to teach.

From that time on, he continued his research while teaching students, but he was teaching others as well. Farmers came to him for help with their crops. Housewives came for advice about their gardens. He was asked to travel to other towns and make speeches about growing things. George was happy at Iowa State and thought he would like to spend the rest of his life there. That did not happen because one day he received a letter.

The letter was from Mr. Booker T. Washington in Alabama. Washington was a former slave too. He was just a few years older than George. He had started a school called Tuskegee Institute. Tuskegee was started to give former slaves and their children an education. Mr. Washington believed that black children needed to go to school and learn the knowledge that is found in books. He also believed that they needed to learn practical skills that would help them make a living. Many black people in those days thought that farming, building, cooking, and other types of physical work were not important things to learn. They thought that those types of work belonged to the old life when they or their parents had been slaves.

Booker told them that all honest work is good. He taught them that they must learn to do things that they could get paid for doing. Then they could raise themselves from poverty and have the time to study any field they wished to learn. So he led them in building their own college.

Tuskegee was still very **primitive**. Booker had started with just some acres of land and some broken-down buildings. He had shown the students that he was willing to work hard and make Tuskegee Institute successful. He set the example by taking off his coat and picking up his tools.

primitive: Not well developed

Together, Booker and his first few students cleared land, built buildings, and planted gardens. They would live in buildings they built for themselves and eat food they had grown themselves. They would make their own clothes and do their own laundry. They would learn how good people feel when they do things and make things that make their lives better.

When George Carver learned what Booker T. Washington was doing for young African Americans, he longed to be a part of Tuskegee. He would spend the rest of his life there.

When George first saw his laboratory, it was an empty room. There was no equipment. There were no worktables. There were no stools on which to sit. So he and his students went searching for things they could use in doing their research. Soon they had collected old bottles, pans, an old oil lamp, some bits of string, and wire. George had a shiny new microscope that his Iowa friends had given him as a going-away gift. With this strange collection, the scientific farming program at Tuskegee began.

The land around Tuskegee was not good for farming. Like much of the South, it had been worn down by years of cotton growing. Cotton was a profitable crop, but it was hard on the land. George Washington Carver understood nature. God had taught him much about soils and about what plants needed from the ground.

He and his students worked and studied. They brought **muck** from the swamps and **compost** from barns to enrich the soil. They found that certain crops such as peanuts and sweet potatoes

muck: Dirty, wet mud

compost: Decayed organic matter used as fertilizer

enriched the soil. George began teaching the farmers in the area how to make their land healthy again by "rotating" their crops. They must not grow cotton every year, he told them. They should plant other crops sometimes.

Farmers were not convinced. They knew they could get money for their cotton and corn. But what would they do with tons of peanuts? Who would want them?

God's Little Workshop

Professor Carver went to work. Spending long, long hours in his laboratory he experimented and tested. He called his lab "God's little workshop" because he depended on the Lord to show him how to study plants. Many times his students would see him bow his head and quietly pray for answers to his questions.

"As I worked on projects which fulfilled a real human need," he would say, "forces were working through me which amazed me. I would often go to sleep with an apparently **insoluble** problem. When I woke the answer was there. Why, then, should we who believe in Christ be so surprised at what God can do with a willing man in a laboratory? Some things must be baffling to the critic who has never been born again."[33]

> **insoluble:**
> Impossible to solve

The answers came. In time, Professor Carver found over 300 uses for peanuts and over 100 uses for sweet potatoes. Now the farmers could help their land by growing less cotton and selling other crops.

George equipped a wagon to go out into the surrounding area and teach the farmers how to farm better. He called it the Jessup wagon because a kind Mr. Jessup had donated the money for it. He spent much time traveling around Tuskegee and beyond, talking about crop rotation, fertilization, and new ways to use the wild plants that grew in the South.

As years went by, he grew more and more famous. He was asked to travel all over the country making speeches about agriculture. He was willing to go, but his favorite place to be was Tuskegee. He loved his students, and he loved the hours spent in his laboratory, working with the great Creator to discover more about how to grow plants and use them.

Once a group of men came to visit Tuskegee and have dinner with Professor Carver. They were men who had donated money to the school because they believed it was important to educate the black young people of the South. George served them a delicious meal. The main course was a chicken dish and there were several interesting side dishes. Dessert was ice cream. After dinner was over, Professor Carver explained that everything they had just eaten was made from peanuts. Even the chicken was not really chicken! The men went away even more eager to help Tuskegee Institute.

George Washington Carver died in 1943, in the middle of World War II. Because of his contributions to science, he was mourned all across America. His birthplace was made a national monument, the first ever to honor a black man. Before he died, Tuskegee established the George Washington Carver Museum at the school to tell about his life and the many things he had discovered and created. When he learned that the museum was to be built in the Institute's old laundry room, he remembered the many hours he had spent washing and ironing to pay for his education. He replied he would like that as he had always felt at home in a laundry.

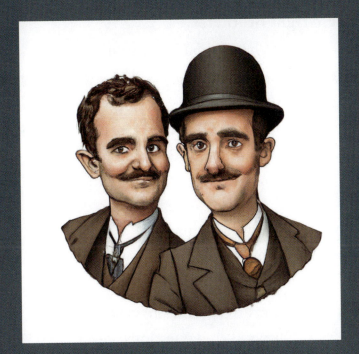

10
The Wright Brothers — Masters of Flight

Orville: 1871–1948
Wilbur: 1867–1912

American aviation pioneers

Who Were the Wright Brothers?

The Wright brothers, Orville Wright and Wilbur Wright were American **aviation** pioneers generally credited with inventing, building, and flying the world's first successful motor-operated airplane. The Wright brothers used intelligence, experience, and ingenuity to design their aircraft. From studying God's creation in the form of bird-flight, they were helped to develop their own creation of a better aircraft. If we marvel at how great their achievement was, how much more should we give glory to the Creator who designed flight in the first place?

> **aviation:** Having to do with airplanes

They were four years apart in age, but they were the best of friends. Always wondering, always asking questions, always making things, the Wright brothers sometimes missed out on some of the neighbor boys' games. But they were having fun in different ways. And while their ways sometimes seemed strange to other children, they would lead Wilbur and Orville down a path that would make both of them world famous and, in fact, change the world itself.

Experiments

Their father, Milton Wright was a traveling preacher, often away from home. But he had a well-equipped workshop out in the family barn which he allowed his sons to use in his absence. Their mother encouraged their experiments, often helping them design projects on paper. "Get it right on paper," Susan Wright would say, "and it will be right when you build it."[34]

The first design Susan created for the boys was a plan for a sled. Will and Orv had been watching the neighbor boys sled down a nearby hill and had taken a few turns going down themselves whenever a friend would grant them a turn. But, of course, they wanted a sled of their own. The other boys had sleds built by their fathers. But Mr. Wright was busy traveling and preaching, so he had little time to do such things.

Will and Orv were not to be denied. "We'll build a sled ourselves," they decided. "And it will be the best sled on this hill!"[35] Home they plodded through the snow, eager to share their plan with their mother. When she heard their scheme, Susan took out a sheet of paper. She was a talented lady with a pencil and paper. Puzzled, the boys watched her. How could anybody build a sled out of paper?

But soon they were looking over her shoulder, sharing their ideas with her and watching her draw a design for each part of the sled. Slowly it began to take shape. Mother suggested that the sled be lower than those of the other boys so that it would have less wind **resistance**. Yes, that would be good. And it would be narrower too, for the same reason. They would make it a little longer than the other boys' sleds, so they could both ride on it and even take along little sister Kate sometimes.

Three days later, the boys emerged from the barn workshop with a brand-new sled. The runners were narrower than those on most sleds so that they would glide more easily through the snow. Also, they had been polished long and hard with sandpaper to make them as smooth as glass. For good measure, the boys had rubbed them with old

> **resistance:** The force that slows down a moving object

candles. This would make them even more slippery in the snow. Now they were ready for the races.

When Will and Orv joined them on the sled hill, they looked at the strange new sled and wondered if it would be any good. One boy **scoffed** that it looked as if it would fall apart if anybody sat on it. When the Wright boys told them that their mother had drawn the design for their sled, they laughed. Who had ever heard of a mother building a sled? Then the race began.

scoffed: Mocked

Both Wilbur and Orville piled onto their sleek, narrow toy. While the other boys sat up straight, the Wright boys laid down as flat as possible. They had not forgotten what their mother had said about wind resistance. Somebody shouted, "Go!" and down the steep hill the racers flew.

Four sleds started out together, but soon it was clear that one was much faster than the rest. Halfway down the hill, Will squinted to get the stinging snow out of his eyes. Where were the other racers? They were not ahead, for he could not see any of them. Turning his head, he saw the other boys a few yards behind. How far back were they? It looked perhaps 20 feet. Then they were 30 feet behind! The little sled skimmed along, its runners slicing through the snow. In just a few seconds it had reached the bottom of the hill where the sleds always stopped. But it didn't stop! On Will and Orv sailed, a hundred yards farther than any of the other boys had gone. Their sled was by far the best on the hill! Better yet, they had learned a great lesson from their mother: design your project well and you will build it well.

The years of boyhood passed on, season after season. The "Bishop's boys," as they were called in the neighborhood, kept on designing and building new things. Their part-time job at the local junkyard supplied them with a little money to buy the materials they needed for their projects, and they often found among the junk things they could use as well. They designed and built a wagon, using wheels from two tricycles that their boss gave them. They used the wagon to collect scrap metal which they sold to the junkyard owner. Now the Wright brothers were independent businessmen.

Again, their creative mother coached the boys on making their invention more effective. When they asked for her advice, she talked about **friction**.

"These wheels are a little too tight on the axles," she said, frowning.

"They're the only axles we could find, Mother," Will answered. "What can we do about it?"

Mother thought a moment. "I don't see how you can get rid of all the friction, but you can lessen it. Try polishing the end of the axle and the inside of the wheel's hub. Then load it with axle grease. That should help."[36]

> **friction:** The resistance that one object encounters when moving over another

It did help. The new wagon was not pretty, but it was easy to pull, even when loaded with junk to sell. Soon the boys were picking up all sorts of metal items that farmers were clearing out of their barns and that their wives were throwing out in spring cleaning. Will and Orv could collect and sell junk to their boss more effectively than ever, and they were making more money to work on their experiments.

One day the brothers decided to buy a kite. Kites were great fun for children and certainly worth the 40 cents each one cost. Soon they were out in the fields on a breezy afternoon with their friends, watching their kites sailing high up on the wind. However, their kites were no better than all the other kites tugging at their strings. Why not try to make a better kite — maybe they could even make one that would lift them into the air with it? The idea stuck with them. It would one day make them famous.

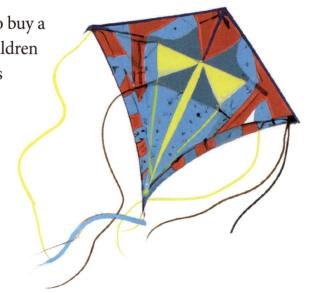

Will and Orv experimented with all sorts of projects as they grew through their teen years. They did indeed build bigger and better kites — though none of them ever lifted the boys off the ground. They designed and built a chair for their mother, using their father's shop tools. While helping their father fold the papers he wrote for the churches, they wondered if they could make a folding machine to do the work for them. Soon, the idea became reality, and they were folding a batch of papers in two hours that had once taken them two days!

Dreams of Flying

In those days, bicycles were becoming popular. Bicycles were new then and were not nearly as light and easy to ride as they are now. Wilbur and Orville opened a bicycle shop and invested their money in buying and fixing broken bikes. As they worked and learned, they dreamed of someday making a machine that would carry them through the sky as a bicycle carried them along the ground. Day after day they improved their mechanical skills as they worked in their shop. And day after day they dreamed of flying.

For centuries, men had dreamed the same exciting dream as the Wright boys did. People had made huge balloons with big baskets hung beneath them for passengers. Stoves were set inside the basket to fill the balloon with hot air. During the Civil War, soldiers used these hot air balloons to spy on enemy armies. People were also experimenting with gliders which looked much like our modern airplanes, with wings to sail through the air and rudders to guide them.

Hot air balloons were hard to steer; the wind took them wherever it happened to be going. Gliders could only stay in the air for a few minutes after sailing off a high hill or cliff. What Will and Orv dreamed of was a flying machine that could stay up in the air as long as its operator might want it to.

In different places around the world, men were working on such machines. The Wright boys joined the crowd of dreamers, focusing their excitement about flight into many different plans. For hours they worked over their designs as their mother had taught them, struggling to "get it right on paper" so that it would be right when they built it. Indeed, this was not just another toy. A man's life would depend on this machine, high up in the air. It had to work.

At last, they were ready to try. They worked with many different kinds of materials to make the wings of their big glider. Some woods were too heavy; some kinds were too weak. Some types of cloth would tear in the wind; some types were coarse and allowed too much air through them. Finally, they were satisfied that their heavier-than-air machine would glide or "soar" as some people called it. However, **launching** it from a hilltop was not in their plans. They needed a motor to pull their machine into the sky.

launching: To set in motion

horseless carriages: Now known as automobiles

Several gasoline-powered motors were being developed around the year 1900. Henry Ford and others were building **"horseless carriages"** and they soon would be common on the city streets. Will and Orv looked at a number of them and read everything they could find about how they worked. By using the mathematic skills they had learned from their brilliant mother, they figured out that no motor of that day would work for their "airplane." They needed a new kind of motor. They needed a motor that had plenty of power but did not weigh so much that it would be hard to lift off the ground with the wings they had built. Here was a very big problem.

The Wright boys were not to be prevented from fulfilling their dream by any problem, large or small. "We'll just have to build our motor ourselves," they agreed. Back to work they went.

Back to Work

Again, it took many long hours and late nights to design and build their newest project. At long last, the Wright engine was finished. They believed it was both light enough and powerful enough to make their airplane fly. One of them would have to risk his life to find out.

The United States Weather Bureau helped them find a place to try their first flight. Kitty Hawk, North Carolina, was a place of steady winds and wide fields where there were no trees. They did not intend to fly very high on their first few flights and trees would have been a great danger.

They experimented first with a **glider** that had no motor. It flew! It actually carried Wilbur a few feet in the air and stayed up a few seconds. Over the next few days, the brothers took turns flying their craft, experimenting with shifting their weight and pulling the **rudder cords** to balance and guide it. With each flight, they learned more about their glider and the effect of the wind on it. They stayed up longer and longer and sailed higher and higher.

The first visit to Kitty Hawk ended with a crash. Will was the pilot that day and was having a wonderful time until a **downdraft** caught the broad wings and sent the glider crashing to the ground. Wilbur lay on the sand, tangled in the wreckage of the machine in which they had invested so much time and money, but he was unhurt. Rushing to him, Orv saw that he was smiling. His brother looked up at him with a gleam in his eye.

glider: A light aircraft that is designed to fly for long periods without using an engine

rudder cords: Rope or cables used to control direction

downdraft: Downwind current of air

"We can build another one, Orv," he said with conviction. "And a better one!"[37]

Sure enough, they did. They returned to Kitty Hawk for another try the following year. This time they applied the lessons they had learned from their failures and built a better glider. On this glider was mounted the Wright gasoline engine, weighing only two hundred pounds and supplying eight **horsepower** of force to the spruce propellers.

This first Wright flying machine did not have wheels. Instead, it had skids underneath that looked like skis. The brothers built two wooden tracks and laid them out on the sandy beach. The machine would slide down these tracks until it gathered enough speed to lift off the ground. On December 17, 1903, Orville won the toss of a coin and took his position on the lower wing of the plane. "I'm going to fly today," he thought as his breath came in gasps and his heart pounded. "I'm going to be the first man in the world to fly."

> **horsepower:** A unit to measure the power an engine produces

Wilbur and a helper started the engine. "You ready, Orv?" he shouted to his brother. He held on to the end of the wing as the glider shook violently.

"All set," Orville yelled back.[38]

"Let her go!" Will commanded, and Orv released the lever that started the propellers biting into the air. Slowly the glider slid down the wooden track. Faster . . . faster yet . . . then the end of the track was rushing toward him, and Orville Wright suddenly realized that he was flying.

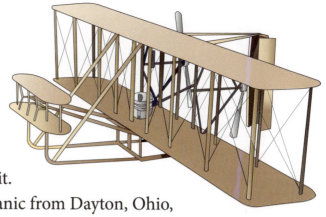

He was sailing along as no man ever had before, just ten feet above the sand, yet feeling as if he were miles up in the sky. Flying! Men had dreamed of it for centuries, but he was doing it. He, Orv Wright, the bike mechanic from Dayton, Ohio, had grown wings.

That first flight only lasted for 12 seconds and 100 feet. Orville slid off the lower wing after landing, and Will took his turn and went 175 feet. Next, Orv went up again and stayed up a few seconds longer than before. Then on his second turn, Will decided to stay up longer. He rose to a height of 20 feet and leveled off. Below him, the sand dunes seemed to be flashing by. The engine throbbed and the flying machine sailed on and on, startling seagulls into screaming flight. This was really flying!

After 800 feet of distance, a down draft forced Will to land. Orv ran to him, panting excitedly.

"You stayed up there 59 seconds! Almost a full minute!"

"Next time," Will answered firmly, "we'll stay up 59 minutes."[39]

All these flying experiments had been conducted in secrecy. At that time in history, few people believed that such flight would ever be possible. It took some time and several more flights before people came to believe that the Wright brothers had actually invented a successful flying machine. But eventually they made believers out of the entire world. Those crazy Wright boys had been "right," after all.

Glossary

apprentice: To work for a skilled craftsman to learn the trade.

aviation: Having to do with airplanes.

bellows: A device with an airbag that blows a stream of air when squeezed.

biblical creationist: A scientist who believed the world was created by God in six days.

boardwalk: A walkway across sand or marshy ground, usually made of wood.

botanist: A plant expert.

Canis familiarus: Dog familiar.

Clermont: Fulton had named the ship, after Clermont, Mr. Livingston's beautiful estate.

compost: Decayed organic matter used as fertilizer.

Diamond Grove: Diamond is located on Diamond Grove Prairie, Missouri.

Dijon Lycée: A secondary school attended before college.

disabled: A condition that limits or creates challenges for a person.

downdraft: Downwind current of air.

dumbstruck: So surprised that one is unable to speak.

electromagnet: A soft metal core made into a magnet by the passage of electric current through a coil surrounding it.

electromagnetism: The branch of physics dealing with the interaction of electric currents.

elocution: The skill of clear and articulate speech.

elocutionist: A public speaker trained in voice production/oratory.

frantically: In a hurried, distraught manner.

friction: The resistance that one object encounters when moving over another.

genius: Exceptional intellectual ability.

glider: A light aircraft that is designed to fly for long periods without using an engine.

horseless carriages: Now known as automobiles.

horsepower: A unit to measure the power an engine produces.

insoluble: Impossible to solve.

intellectually: Related to how a person's brain works.

jeer: Make rude and mocking remarks.

jovial: Cheerful and friendly.

Lapland: A region in northern Norway, northern Sweden, and Northern Finland.

launching: To set in motion.

loathsome: Repulsive or disgusting.

meteor: A shooting star.

microbiology: The branch of science that deals with microorganisms.

modest: Humble.

Morse code: An alphabet or code in which letters are represented by combinations of long and short signals of light or sound.

muck: Dirty, wet mud.

musket: An infantryman's light gun with a long barrel, typically smooth-bored, muzzleloading, and fired from the shoulder.

mythological: Lacking factual basis or historical validity.

pasteboard: A type of thin board made by pasting together sheets of paper.

patents: Legal documents protecting an inventor's right to profit from his inventions.

phosphorous: A poisonous, combustible substance that ignites easily in the air.

primitive: Not well developed.

prominent: Famous, important.

resistance: The force that slows down a moving object.

Royal Academy: A society founded in 1768 by George III of England for the establishment of a school of design which held an annual exhibition of the works of living artists.

rudder cords: Rope or cables used to control direction.

scanty: Very, very little.

scoffed: Mocked.

Seine: A river in France.

smith: Blacksmith.

swine: Pig.

tanner: A person who tans animal hides to create leather.

tapered off: Slowed down.

telegraph: A system for transmitting messages from a distance along a wire.

Tory: American colonist who supported the British side.

trademark: A symbol or word legally registered to represent a company.

transmitters: Equipment used to generate and send messages.

type: Physical letters used to make words for a newspaper to be printed from.

upstart: Not afraid to try new things.

verdure: Vegetation.

witty: Quick and inventive humor.

Yale College: Today's Yale University in New Haven, Connecticut.

Corresponding Curriculum

The *What a Character! Series* can be used alongside Master Books curriculum for reading practice or to dive deeper on topics that are of special interest to students. We have provided this list to help match the book topics with Master Books curriculum.

This book in the series features famous inventors and scientists, whose stories would incorporate well for students in grades 4–8 with history, language arts vocabulary words and definitions, as well as science, innovation, and cultural insights.

Chapter 1: Carl Linnaeus — The Boy Who Loved Plants

Design for Life

Design for Heaven and Earth

Language Lessons for a Living Education

World Geography and Cultures

Elementary World History

Chapter 2: Eli Whitney — Creative Inventor

America's Story — Volume 2

Language Lessons for a Living Education

Chapter 3: Robert Fulton — Inventor of the Steamboat

Language Lessons for a Living Education

America's Story Volume 2

World Geography and Cultures

Chapter 4: Samuel F.B. Morse — A Man Who Wrote with Lightning

America's Story — Volume 2

Language Lessons for a Living Education

Chapter 5: Louis Pasteur — The Boy Who Asked Questions

Design for the Heavens and Earth *Elementary World History*
Language Lessons for a Living Education *World Geography and Cultures*

Chapter 6: Alexander Graham Bell and the Talking Machine

America's Story Volume 2 *World Geography and Cultures*
Language Lessons for A Living Education *Elementary World History*

Chapter 7: Thomas Edison — Just the Strange Boy the World Needed

America's Story — Volume 2 *Design for Life*
Language Lessons for a Living Education

Chapter 8: Booker T. Washington — From Slave to Scientist

America's Story — Volume 2 or 3 *Language Lessons for a Living Education*

Chapter 9: George Washington Carver — God's Plant Doctor

Design for Life *Language Lessons for a Living Education*
America's Story — Volume 2 or 3

Chapter 10: The Wright Brothers — Masters of Flight

America's Story — Volume 3 *Language Lessons for a Living Education*

Endnotes

1. Carl Linnaeus, translated by Charles Troilus and James Edward Smith, *A Tour in Lapland* (Ex-classics Project, 2021), 192, https://www.exclassics.com/lachesis/lachesis.pdf.
2. *Carl Linnaeus, Botanist, physician, scientist, Zoologist* prabook.com, January 17, 2023, https://prabook.com/web/carl.linnaeus/3732317.
3. Linnaeus, *A Tour in Lapland*, 238.
4. Frances M. Perry, *Four American Inventors* (New York: American Book Company, 1901), 77.
5. Ibid., 79.
6. Ibid., 93.
7. Ibid., 96–97.
8. Frances M. Perry, *Four American Inventors* (New York: American Book Company, 1901), 11.
9. Ibid., 12.
10. Ibid., 13.
11. Ibid., 49.
12. Ibid., 52
13. J.H. Tiner, *Samuel F.B. Morse — Artist with a Message* (Milford, MI: Mott Media, 1987), p. 116.
14. Frances M. Perry, *Four American Inventors* (New York: American Book Company, 1901), 152.
15. Ibid., 154–155.
16. Tiner, *Samuel F.B. Morse—Artist with a Message*, p. 116.
17. Perry, *Four American Inventors*, 187–189.
18. Ibid., 191.
19. *The Literary Digest* (October 18, 1902) https://archive.org/details/literarydigest24newy.
20. Elizabeth Rider Montgomery, *Alexander Graham Bell: Man of Sound* (Champaign, IL: Garrard Publishing Co., 1963), 15.
21. Ibid., 18
22. Ibid., 20.
23. Katherine Shippen, *Mr. Bell Invents the Telephone* (New York: Random House, 1952), 46.
24. Montgomery, *Alexander Graham Bell: Man of Sound*, 54.
25. Frances M. Perry, *Four American Inventors* (New York: American Book Company, 1901), 210.
26. Ibid., 211.
27. Booker T. Washington, *Up From Slavery: An Autobiography* (Mineola, NY: Dover Publications, Inc., 1995).
28. Ibid., 125.
29. Ibid.
30. George Washington Carver, *George Washington Carver Quotes*, https://quotefancy.com/george-washington-carver-quotes, January 17, 2023.
31. Gary R. Kremer, ed. *George Washington Carver: In His Own Words* (Columbia, MO: University of Missouri Press, 2017), 160.
32. Ibid., 146.
33. Ibid., 162.
34. Quentin Reynolds, *The Wright Brothers: Pioneers of American Aviation* (New York: Random House, 1950), 15.
35. Ibid., 11.
36. Ibid., 39.
37. Ibid., 144.
38. Ibid., 164.
39. Ibid., 167.

A CLASSIC PRESENTATION OF GOD'S REDEMPTIVE PLAN FOR MANKIND

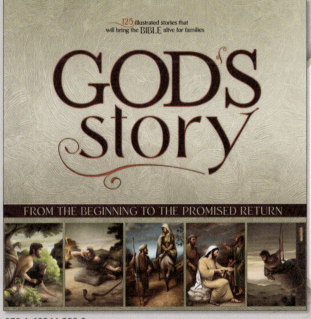

978-1-68344-288-2

This beautifully illustrated book of Bible stories will delight both children and adults! Enjoy short, easy-to-read examples of God's transforming power in the lives of biblical believers and skeptics. Revisit the moments that reveal God's love for us — from the Fall in the Garden of Eden, to the judgement of the Flood, the trials and triumphs of Israel, and the promise of a Savior, through doubt, rebellion, and despair, these events lead us to the gift of Christ among us and the promise of eternity with God.

spreads from the book

Master Books®
A Division of New Leaf Publishing Group
www.masterbooks.com

What a Character!
READER'S FOR KIDS
Notable Lives from History

Inspire Students with Biographies of Notable Lives from HISTORY.

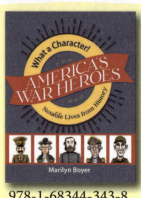

978-1-68344-343-8

978-1-68344-342-1

MasterBooks.co
Where Faith Grows!